Table of Contents

Unit 1 Vowel sound /a/, /e/ 3
Unit 2 Vowels /i/, /o/, /u/ 10
Unit 3 Vowels /a/, /e/, /i/, /o/, /u/ 17
Unit 4 Vowel /u/, /oo/ 24
Unit 5 Vowel /ə/ 32
Unit 6 Review tests 243-250

Unit 7 Vowel / ã/ 40
Unit 8 Vowel /ē/ 47
Unit 9 Vowel / ī/ 54
Unit 10 Vowels /ō/, /ū/ 61
Unit 11 Vowels /ā/, /ē/, /ī/, /ō/, / ū/ 68
Unit 12 Review tests 251-258

Unit 13 R-controlled vowels / är/, /ãr/, or /er/ 76
Unit 14 R-controlled vowels /ēr/, / ər/, /ur/ 83
Unit 15 R-controlled vowel /ôr/ 90
Unit 16 R-controlled vowel /ėr/ 97
Unit 17 R-controlled vowel /ər/ 104
Unit 18 Review tests 259-266

Unit 19 Initial **kn**, **wr**, **gu** 112
Unit 20 Silent letters 119
Unit 21 Digraphs **qu**, **squ** 126
Unit 22 Consonant clusters **str**, **scr** 133
Unit 23 Consonant clusters **ld**, **nd**, **nk** 140
Unit 24 Review tests 267-274

Unit 25 Irregular plurals 148
Unit 26 Plurals 155
Unit 27 Suffixes **ed**, **ing** 162
Unit 28 Suffixes **ed**, **ing** 169
Unit 29 Suffixes **er**, **est** 176
Unit 30 Review tests 275-282

Unit 31 Contractions 184
Unit 32 Homophones 191
Unit 33 Consonant digraph **ph** 198
Unit 34 Suffixes **able**, **ance**, **age**, **en**, **some** 202
Unit 35 Suffixes **ment**, **ful**, **ness**, **less** 212
Unit 36 Review tests 283-290

Spelling Glossary 219
Answer Key.. 292-327

It is recommended to remove the answer key and unit tests before book is given to the student. The plans for this book is one page per day Monday through Wednesday. Thursday's work is writing the words three times each. The test is to be given on Friday. Review tests are provided for every sixth unit. The recommendation for unit tests is to give one per day.

Grace and Glory Curriculum
written by
Victoria Kays

Unit 1

This lesson has words with the short **a** and short **e** sounds.

1. crack
2. damp
3. animal
4. travel
5. camel
6. planet
7. grand
8. every
9. never
10. address
11. pest
12. pepper
13. mend
14. lemon

The short **a** is the vowel sound you hear in **cat** and **camp**. The short **e** is the vowel sound you hear in **met** and **men**. The short e sound can also be spelled by the letters **ea** such as in **weather**.

Unit 1

1. crack
2. damp
3. animal
4. travel
5. camel
6. planet
7. grand

8. every
9. never
10. address
11. pest
12. pepper
13. mend
14. lemon

A. Write the spelling words that have the short **a** vowel sound.
One word has a short **a** sound and a short **e** sound.

1. _____ 2. _____

3. _____ 4. _____

5. _____ 6. _____

7. _____ 8. _____

B. Write the spelling words that have the short **e** vowel sound.
One word has a short **a** sound and a short **e** sound.

1. _____ 2. _____

3. _____ 4. _____

5. _____ 6. _____

7. _____

C. Vowel letters are missing from these spelling words. Fill in the missing letters.

1. cr ___ck   2. c ___m ___l

3. d ___mp   4. ___n ___m ___l

5. tr ___v ___l   6. l ___mon

7. m ___nd   8. ___v ___ry

9. n ___ver   10. ___ddr ___ss

11. p ___st   12. p ___pp ___r

13. pl ___n ___t   14. gr ___nd

A. Write the spelling word for each pronunciation.

1. (pĕp' ər) _____

2. (nĕv' ər) _____

3. (plăn' ĭt) _____

4. (crăk) _____

5. (ăn' ə məl) _____

6. (ĕv' rē) _____

B. Find these words in your spelling glossary. Write the part of speech for each word.

1. address _____ 2. damp _____

3. mend _____ 4. camel _____

5. grand _____ 6. planet _____

C. Write a spelling word for each definition.

1. to go from one place to another _____

2. at no time _____

3. a desert animal with humps _____

4. a street and house number _____

5. a little wet _____

6. to repair or fix _____

Fill in the blanks with spelling words. You will need to add **ed** to one word.

A (1)_____can be a very useful

(2)_____, or it can be a (3)_____.

It is useful to (4)_____across deserts on our

(5)_____. The camel does not need to live where

it is (6)_____because its body stores water. A camel

(7)_____ learns to love its master.

A (8)_____is a small, yellow citrus fruit.

They are peeled, not (9)_____. Not

(10)_____person likes drinks made from

these fruits. Lemon (11)_____can be sprinkled on

hamburgers to give them a (12)_____taste.

Write the spelling words three times.

1. crack _____   _____

   _____

2. damp _____   _____

   _____

3. animal _____   _____

   _____

4. travel _____   _____

   _____

5. camel _____   _____

   _____

6. planet _____   _____

   _____

7. grand _____   _____

   _____

8. every _____   _____

   _____

9. never _____   _____

   _____

10. address _____   _____

    _____

11. pest   _____   _____

    _____

12. pepper   _____   _____

    _____

13. mend   _____   _____

    _____

14. lemon   _____   _____

    _____

Unit 2

This lesson has words with the short **i, o,** and **u** sounds.

1. mist
2. rich
3. sink
4. silk
5. mittens
6. undone
7. bunch
8. strum
9. rumble
10. socks
11. robin
12. doctor
13. topcoat
14. copper

The short **i** is the vowel sound you hear in **kit**. The short **u** is the vowel sound you hear in **cut**. The short **o** is the vowel sound you hear in **cot**. The short vowel sounds in these words are spelled by single vowel letters.

Unit 2

1. mist
2. rich
3. sink
4. silk
5. mittens
6. undone
7. bunch
8. strum
9. rumble
10. socks
11. robin
12. doctor
13. topcoat
14. copper

A. Write the spelling words that have the short **i** sound.

1. _____   2._____

3. _____   4._____

5. _____

B. Write the spelling words that have the short **o** sound.

1. _____   2._____

3. _____   4._____

5. _____

C. Write the spelling words that have the short **u** sound.

1. _____   2._____

3. _____   4._____

D. Write the spelling words that rhyme with each of these words.

1. milk _____

2. rocks _____

3. kittens _____

4. tumble _____

E. Vowel letters are missing from these spelling words. Fill in the missing letters.

1. ___d ___ne   2. c ___pp ___r

3. d ___ct ___r   4. t___pc___ ___t

12

A. Write the spelling word for each dictionary pronunciation.

   1. (singk) _____

   2. (rŏb′ ən) _____

   3. (dŏk′ tər) _____

   4. (rŭm′ bəl) _____

B. Words that are opposite in meaning are called **antonyms**. For example the words **in** and **out** are antonyms. Write the spelling word that is an antonym for each of these words.

   1. poor _____ 2. done _____

C. Write each spelling word in syllables using hyphens between the syllables. Use your spelling glossary if you need help.

   1. mittens_____

   2. undone_____

   3. rumble _____

   4. robin_____

   5. doctor_____

   6. topcoat_____

   7. copper _____

Write the word or words for each definition.

1. articles of clothing _____

   _____   _____

2. a person who prescribes medicine for sick people _____

3. a light rain _____

4. a large group of things _____

5. a kind of metal used for water pipes _____

6. a kind of cloth _____

7. not finished _____

8. a kind of bird _____

9. not poor _____

10. a low, heavy continuous sound _____

11. a basin used for washing things _____

Write the spelling words three times.

1. mist _____ _____

_____

2. rich _____ _____

_____

3. sink _____ _____

_____

4. silk _____ _____

_____

5. mittens _____ _____

_____

6. undone _____ _____

_____

7. bunch _____ _____

_____

8. strum _____ _____

_____

10. socks _____   _____

_____

11. robin _____   _____

_____

12. doctor _____   _____

_____

13. topcoat _____ _____

_____

14. copper _____   _____

_____

Unit 3

This lesson has words with the short **a, e, i, o u** sounds.

1. liver
2. chicken
3. tennis
4. cabin
5. similar
6. ladder
7. hundred
8. empty
9. leather
10. basket
11. stock
12. puppet
13. pocket
14. summer

The short **a** is the vowel sound you hear in **mat**. The short **e** is the vowel sound you hear in **red**. The short **i** is the vowel sound you hear in **hit**. The short **o** is the vowel sound you hear in **rod**. The short **u** is the vowel sound you hear in **pup**. The short **e** can also be spelled by the letters **ea** such as in **weather**.

Unit 3

1. liver
2. chicken
3. tennis
4. cabin
5. similar
6. ladder
7. hundred
8. empty
9. leather
10. basket
11. stock
12. puppet
13. pocket
14. summer

A. Write the spelling words that have the short **a** sound in the first syllable.

1. _____ 2. _____

3. _____

B. Write the spelling words that have the short **i** sound in the first syllable.

1. _____ 2. _____

3. _____

C. Write the spelling words that have the short **o** sound in the first syllable or the only syllable.

1. _____ 2. _____

D. Write the spelling words and that have the short **e** sound in the first syllable.

1. _____ 2. _____

3. _____

E. Write the spelling words and that have the short **u** sound in the first syllable.

1. _____ 2. _____

3. _____

F. Write the spelling words that have double consonants.

1. _____ 2. _____

3. _____ 4. _____

A. Write the part of speech for each spelling word.

1. liver _____

2. cabin _____

3. chicken _____

4. pocket _____

B. Find the misspelled word in each set. Write it correctly.

1. empty, summer, tenis _____

2. leether, hundred, basket _____

3. similar, stok, puppet _____

C. Write each spelling word in syllables using hyphens between the syllables. Use your spelling dictionary if you need help.

1. ladder _____

2. basket _____

3. summer _____

4. similar _____

5. empty _____

6. puppet _____

7. hundred _____

Fill in the blanks with spelling words. You will need to add **s** to one word.

1. _____ is a good time to go camping.

2. Bake some _____ to take with you.

3. Pack it in a _____.

4. You could play _____ in the daytime.

5. You can sleep in a _____ at night.

6. Make sure you put your keys in your _____.

7. Take some _____ along because children might want to play with them.

8. _____ up on batteries for a flashlight.

9. Take one _____ dollars with you.

10. Take a _____ if you plan to climb a tree.

11. You will not need a _____ jacket.

12. Take your basket home when it's _____.

13. This trip will be _____ to a picnic.

Write the spelling words three times.

1. liver

2. chicken

3. tennis

4. cabin

5. similar

6. ladder

7. hundred

8. empty

9. leather

10. basket _____   _____

   _____

11. stock _____   _____

   _____

12. puppet _____   _____

   _____

13. pocket _____   _____

   _____

14. summer _____   _____

   _____

Unit 4

This lesson has words with the vowel sound you hear in the word **full**. The letters **oo**, **ou**, and **u** are used to make this sound.

1. plural
2. put
3. full
4. shook
5. hood
6. brook
7. should
8. foot
9. wool
10. took
11. footstep
12. woodchuck
13. book
14. childhood

Unit 4

1. plural
2. put
3. full
4. shook
5. hood
6. brook
7. should
8. foot
9. wool
10. took
11. footstep
12. woodchuck
13. book
14. childhood

A. Write the spelling words and that spell the vowel sound you hear in **push** with a **u**.

1. _____   2. _____

3. _____

B. Vowel letters are missing from these spelling words and Extra Words. Fill in the missing letters.

1. h _____ d   2. f _____ t

3. w _____ l   4. sh _____ d

C. Write the spelling words that end with **ook**.

1. _____   2. _____

3. _____   4. _____

D. Write the spelling words that have two syllables.

1. _____   2. _____

3. _____

E. Write the spelling word that completes each sentence.

1. A _____ is a small stream.

2. A _____ is a small, furry animal with a bushy tail.

3. A _____ is something to read.

A. Find each word in your spelling dictionary. Write the part of speech for each word.

1. full _____   2. foot _____

3. shook _____   4. brook _____

5. wool _____   6. took _____

B. Write the words in each set in alphabetical order.

1. took, plural, hood _____   _____

_____

2. childhood, shook, brook   _____

_____

_____

3. wool, put, foot_____   _____

_____

4. took, full, book _____

_____

5. woodchuck, took, shook _____   _____

_____

6. should, footstep, plural_____

_____   _____

A. Write a spelling word for each definition.

1. a small stream _____

2. more than one _____

3. trembled _____

4. the time from birth to adulthood _____

5. the step of walking _____

6. a small, furry animal _____

B. Write a spelling word to complete each sentence.

1. Please _____ the pans in the cabinet.

2. Do you have a sweater with a _____ on it?

3. Was the milk jug completely _____?

4. I bought him some _____ pants.

5. I want to finish reading the _____.

6. _____ you do your homework first?

7. James _____ pictures with his camera.

8. James's _____ was broken.

Write the spelling words three times.

1. plural _____   _____

   _____

2. put _____   _____

   _____

3. full _____   _____

   _____

4. shook _____   _____

   _____

5. hood _____   _____

   _____

6. brook _____   _____

   _____

7. should _____   _____

   _____

8. foot _____   _____

   _____

9. wool _____   _____

   _____

10. took _____ _____

_____

11. footstep _____ _____

_____

12. woodchuck _____

_____

_____

13. book _____ _____

_____

14. childhood _____

_____

_____

Unit 5

This lesson has words with a **schwa** sound. The **schwa** sounds much like a short **u**. It can be spelled with any of the vowels. It is usually found in the syllable that does not have an accent mark on it. In the dictionary pronunciation, the **schwa** looks like ə.

1. away
2. wagon
3. among
4. eleven
5. silent
6. pencil
7. across
8. garage
9. celery
10. parent
11. careful
12. family
13. number
14. oven

Unit 5

1. away
2. wagon
3. among
4. eleven
5. silent
6. pencil
7. across
8. garage
9. celery
10. parent
11. careful
12. family
13. number
14. oven

A. Write the spelling words that have the schwa sound spelled by the letter **a**.

1. _____   2. _____

3. _____   4. _____

B. Write the spelling words that have the schwa sound spelled by the letter **e**.

1. _____   2. _____

3. _____   4. _____

C. Write the spelling words that have the schwa sound spelled by the letter **i**.

1. _____   2. _____

D. Write the spelling word that has the schwa sound spelled by the letter **o**.

_____

E. Write the spelling words with three syllables.

1. _____   2. _____

3. _____

F. Fill in the missing letters that spell the **schwa** sound in these words.

1. caref ___ l   2. wag ___ n

3. penc ___ l   4. sil ___ nt

5. cel ___ ry   6. ov ___ n

A. Write the spelling word for each pronunciation.

1. (nŭm′ bər) _____

2. (pãr′ ənt) _____

3. (sĕl′ ər ē) _____

4. (kãr′ fəl) _____

5. (ə wā′) _____

6. (făm′ ə lē) _____

B. Words that are almost the same are **synonyms**. Write a spelling word that is a synonym for each of these words.

1. quiet _____

2. cart _____

3. numeral _____

C. Find the misspelled word in east set. Write the word correctly.

1. celery, amung, parent _____

2. elven, careful, number _____

3. wagon, acros, away _____

4. parent, ovin, garage _____

5. carful, again, garage _____

A. Write a spelling word that fits each definition.

1. _____ a writing utensil

2. _____ one more than ten

3. _____ a mother or father

4. _____ a group of people related to each other

5. _____ a place to keep a car

6. _____ totally quiet

B. Use spelling words to complete the sentences.

1. I baked a cake in the _____.

2. James likes to put peanut butter in his _____.

3. He drove _____ to street to the restaurant.

4. Sometimes it's good to go _____ for a vacation.

5. We went for a hayride in a _____.

6. Twenty-three is a _____.

7. Be _____ when riding a bike on the road.

8. Which student was the tallest _____ the eight of them?

Write the spelling words three times.

1. away _____ _____

   _____

2. wagon _____ _____

   _____

3. among _____ _____

   _____

4. eleven _____ _____

   _____

5. silent _____ _____

   _____

6. pencil _____ _____

   _____

7. across _____ _____

   _____

8. garage _____ _____

   _____

9. celery _____ _____

   _____

10. parent _____   _____

   _____

11. careful _____   _____

   _____

12. family _____   _____

   _____

13. number _____   _____

   _____

14. oven _____   _____

   _____

Unit 6
Review tests

Ask teacher for test.

Part 1 Grade _____

Part 2 Grade _____

Part 3 Grade _____

Part 4 Grade _____

Unit 7

This lesson has words with the long **a** sound.

1. skate
2. trade
3. stage
4. daylight
5. brain
6. railroad
7. remain
8. raise
9. pain
10. stray
11. rays
12. lace
13. steak
14. break

These spelling words have the long **a** sound. The long **a** is the vowel sound you hear in **day**. The long **a** sound can be spelled by **ay**, **ai**, **ea**, and the **a** consonant **e** pattern.

Unit 7

1. skate
2. trade
3. stage
4. daylight
5. brain
6. railroad
7. remain

8. raise
9. pain
10. stray
11. rays
12. lace
13. steak
14. break

A. Write the spelling words that have the long **a** vowel sound spelled by the
   a + **consonant** + **e** spelling pattern.

   1. _____   2. _____

   3. _____   4. _____

B. Write the spelling words that have the long **a** vowel sound spelled
   by the letters **ay**.

   1. _____   2. _____

   3. _____

C. Write the spelling words that have the long **a** vowel sound spelled by the
   letters **ai**.

   1. _____   2. _____

   3. _____   4. _____

   5. _____

D. Write the spelling words that have the long **a** vowel sound spelled by the
   letters **ea**.

   1. _____   2. _____

E. Vowels are missing in these words. Fill in the missing vowels.

   1. br ____ n   2. st ___ ___ k

   3. d ____ l ___ ght   4. r ___ ___ s ___

   5. br _ ___ k   6. l ___ c ___

   7. r _____ ___ l r _____ d   8. sk _____ t ___

41

A. Write each spelling word in syllables using hyphens between the syllables. Use your spelling dictionary if you need help.

1. remain _____

2. daylight _____

3. railroad _____

B. Words that sound the same but are spelled differently and have different meanings are called **homophones**. For example, **hear** and **here** are homophones. Write a spelling word that is a homophone for each word.

1. rays _____

2. brake _____

3. stake _____

4. pane _____

C. Find the misspelled word in each set.

1. traid, skate, steak _____

2. railroad, break, scate _____

3. daylite, remain, raise _____

4. raise, staje, break _____

5. strai, brain, trade _____

6. stage, pain, lase _____

Write the spelling word for each definition.

1. to stay in a place _____

2. an ache _____

3. the body's chief nerve center _____

4. thin beams of light _____

5. a dog or cat with no home _____

6. the time we see the light from the sun _____

7. to damage by tearing or cracking _____

8. a shoe with wheels or a blade _____

9. an open weaving or net of fine thread in an ornamental pattern used for decorations _____

10. an exchange of one thing for another _____

11. to lift up _____

12. one step or degree in a process _____

13. a system that runs trains _____

14. a cut of meat _____

 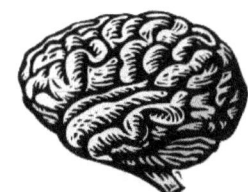 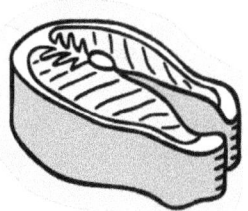

Write the spelling words three times.

1. skate _____ _____

   _____

2. trade _____ _____

   _____

3. stage _____ _____

   _____

4. daylight _____ _____

   _____

5. brain _____ _____

   _____

6. railroad _____ _____

   _____

7. remain _____ _____

   _____

8. raise _____ _____

   _____

9. pain _____ _____

   _____

10. stray _____ _____

_____

11. rays _____ _____

_____

12. lace _____ _____

_____

13. steak _____ _____

_____

14. break _____ _____

_____

Unit 8

This lesson has words with the long **e** sound.

1. honey
2. money
3. key
4. monkey
5. handy
6. silly
7. freeze
8. leaf
9. gleam
10. agree
11. please
12. speed
13. cream
14. pony

The long **e** is the vowel sound you hear in **bee**. The long **e** sound can be spelled by **ey**, **y**, **ee**, and **ea**.

Unit 8

1. honey
2. money
3. key
4. monkey
5. handy
6. silly
7. freeze
8. leaf
9. gleam
10. agree
11. please
12. speed
13. cream
14. pony

A. Write the spelling words in which the letters **ee** spell the long **e** sound.

1. _____   2. _____

3. _____

B. Write the spelling words in which the letters **ea** spell the long **e** sound.

1. _____   2. _____

3. _____   4. _____

C. Write the spelling words in which the letters **ey** spell the long **e** sound.

1. _____   2. _____

3. _____   4. _____

D. Write the spelling words in which the letter **y** spells the long **e** sound.

1. _____   2. _____

3. _____

E. Vowels are missing in these words. Fill in the missing vowels.

1. h ___ n _____   2. gl ___ ___m

3. m ___nk _____   4. ___gr___ ___

5. fr _____ z ___   6. m ___n _____

7. pl _____ s ___   8. cr _____ m

9. h ___nd ___   10. s ___ll ___

48

A. Write the spelling word for each definition.

1. to shine or be bright _____

2. foolish _____

3. the part of milk that contains butterfat _____

4. to have the same opinion _____

5. to make someone happy _____

6. an animal that looks like a small ape _____

7. fast movement _____

B. One word in each set is misspelled. Write it correctly.

1. honey, ponny, handy _____

2. freaze, money, leaf _____

3. key, monkey, huney _____

4. gleam, speed, muney _____

5. leef, handy, agree _____

C. Write a sentence using the word **key**.

_____

_____

Fill in the blanks with spelling words. You will need to add **s** to one word.

1. Bees make _____ that we can eat.

2. You can see _____ swinging from ropes at the zoo.

3. Please slow your _____ in a school zone.

4. Do not act _____ in school.

5. Do you _____ with the president?

6. Fred could ride his small _____.

7. Jimmy and David counted their _____ from their banks.

8. Water will _____ if the temperature drops below 32 degrees Fahrenheit.

9. James likes to eat ice _____.

10. A green _____ may turn yellow or orange in the fall.

11. I was using the wrong _____ to open the lock.

12. Benjamin had a _____ on his face after seeing his mother.

13. _____ listen to the presidential debate.

14. A screwdriver is a _____ tool to use.

Write the spelling words three times.

1. honey

2. money

3. key

4. monkey

5. handy

6. silly

7. freeze

8. leaf

9. gleam

10. agree _____   _____

   _____

11. please _____   _____

   _____

12. speed _____   _____

   _____

13. cream _____   _____

   _____

14. pony _____   _____

   _____

Unit 9

This lesson has words with the long **i** sound.

1. pilot
2. pile
3. surprise
4. alive
5. sight
6. height
7. tiny
8. flight
9. tonight
10. siren
11. quiet
12. guide
13. supplies
14. qualified

The long **i** is the vowel sound you hear in **ice**. The long **i** sound can be spelled by an **i**, **eigh**, **igh**, **ie,** and the **i** consonant **e** pattern.

Unit 9

1. pilot
2. pile
3. surprise
4. alive
5. sight
6. height
7. tiny
8. flight
9. tonight
10. siren
11. quiet
12. guide
13. supplies
14. qualified

A. Write the spelling words that have the long **i** vowel sound spelled by the **i + consonant + e** spelling pattern.

   1. _____   2. _____

   3. _____   4. _____

B. Write the spelling words that have the long **i** vowel sound spelled by the letters **igh**.

   1. _____   2. _____

   3. _____

C. Write the spelling words that have the long **i** vowel sound spelled by the letter **i**.

   1. _____   2. _____

   3. _____   4. _____

D. Write the spelling words that have the long **i** vowel sound spelled by the letters **ie**.

   1. _____   2. _____

E. Write the word that has the long **i** sound spelled by the letters **eigh**.

   _____

F. Vowels are missing in these words. Fill in the missing vowels.

   1. qu___ ___ t   2. qualif ___ ___d

   3. suppl___ ___ s   4. gu ___ d ___

   5. s___ ght   6. h ___ ___ ght

A. Write each spelling word in syllables using hyphens between the syllables. Use your spelling dictionary if you need help.

1. pilot _____

2. surprise _____

3. alive _____

4. tiny _____

5. tonight _____

6. siren _____

7. quiet _____

8. supplies _____

9. qualified_____

B. Write these words in alphabetical order.

| surprise | height | tiny | sight | flight |
| qualified | siren | guide | quiet | tonight |

1. _____ 6. _____

2. _____ 7. _____

3. _____ 8. _____

4. _____ 9. _____

5. _____ 10. _____

Complete the story with spelling words. You will need to add an **s** to two words.

Are you afraid of (1) _____? If so, you would not make a good (2) _____.

Wilbur and Orville Wright wanted to make a flying machine. They gathered (3) _____ to make a plane. They needed someone to (4) _____ them. They also needed to have good eye (5) _____. Some of their (6) _____ were not successful. One night Orville lay awake when it was (7) _____ and tried to think what they could do to make their plane fly better. It would be nice to (8) _____ everyone by showing them how their machine could fly. He didn't want it to end up being a (9) _____ of metal. He also wanted to stay (10) _____. Neither one of the boys wanted to hear a (11) _____ from an ambulance coming to their rescue. They finally were able to make their plane fly, but they would not be (12) _____ to fly a plane today. Their plane would be considered (13) _____ compared to planes today.

Do you want to fly a plane (14) _____?

Write the spelling words three times.

1. pilot _____   _____

   _____

2. pile _____   _____

   _____

3. surprise _____   _____

   _____

4. alive _____   _____

   _____

5. sight _____   _____

   _____

6. height _____   _____

   _____

7. tiny _____   _____

   _____

8. flight _____   _____

   _____

9. tonight _____   _____

   _____

10. siren   _____   _____

             _____

11. quiet   _____   _____

             _____

12. guide   _____   _____

             _____

13. supplies _____   _____

             _____

14. qualified _____   _____

             _____

Unit 10

This lesson has words with the long **o** sound and the long **u** sound.

1. piano
2. spoke
3. groan
4. know
5. oak
6. gold
7. post

8. huge
9. cute
10. below
11. use
12. over
13. bone
14. abuse

    The long **o** is the vowel sound you hear in **sold**. The long **o** sound can be spelled by an **o**, **oa**, **ow**, and the **o** consonant **e** pattern. The long **u** sound is the vowel sound you hear in **use**. The long **u** words in this lesson follow the **u** + **consonant** + **e** pattern.

Unit 10

1. piano
2. spoke
3. groan
4. know
5. oak
6. gold
7. post
8. huge
9. cute
10. below
11. use
12. over
13. bone
14. abuse

A. Write the spelling words that have the long **o** vowel sound spelled by the **o** + **consonant** + **e** spelling pattern.

1. _____ 2. _____

B. Write the spelling words that have the long **o** vowel sound spelled by the letters **oa**.

1. _____ 2. _____

C. Write the spelling words that have the long **o** vowel sound spelled by the letters **ow**.

1. _____ 2. _____

D. Write the spelling words that have the long **o** vowel sound spelled by the letter **o**.

1. _____ 2. _____

3. _____ 4. _____

E. Write the spelling words that have the long **u** vowel sound spelled by the **u** + **consonant** + **e** spelling pattern.

1. _____ 2. _____

3. _____ 4. _____

F. Write spelling words that rhyme with each of these words.

1. host _____ 2. cold _____

3. mute _____ 4. moan _____

A. Write the spelling word for each dictionary pronunciation.

1. (ō′ vər) _____ 2. (bōn) _____

3. (grōn) _____ 4. (ōk) _____

5. (bĭ lō′) _____ 6. (spōk) _____

7. (gōld) _____ 8. (pōst) _____

B. One word in each set is misspelled. Write the word correctly.

1. below, huje, over _____

2. kno, use, cute _____

3. abuse, gold, peano _____

4. kute, spoke, huge _____

5. uze, piano, groan _____

6. bone, oak, ubuse _____

C. Find the part of speech for each word. Use your spelling glossary.

1. piano _____

2. over _____

3. groan _____

4. below _____

5. use _____

6. bone _____

Complete the sentences with spelling words. You will need to add **ed** to one word.

1. Abigail and Monica are _____little girls.

2. James was tuning the _____.

3. An elephant is a _____animal.

4. Turn your paper _____and read the other side.

5. I _____to Clara about the situation.

6. She did not _____ the child.

7. The mandible is a _____ in the jaw.

8. I do not _____ how to rebuild an engine.

9. James drove the fence _____into the ground.

10. The umbrella was lying _____the seat.

11. I _____because I was having so much pain.

12. A _____watch would be expensive.

13. _____a pencil when writing on the test paper.

14. _____is a hard wood.

64

Write the spelling words three times.

1. piano _____ _____

   _____

2. spoke _____ _____

   _____

3. groan _____ _____

   _____

4. know _____ _____

   _____

5. oak _____ _____

   _____

6. gold _____ _____

   _____

7. post _____ _____

   _____

8. huge _____ _____

   _____

9. cute _____ _____

   _____

10. below _____ _____

_____

11. use _____ _____

_____

12. over _____ _____

_____

13. bone _____ _____

_____

14. abuse _____ _____

_____

Unit 11

This lesson has words with the all the long vowel sounds.

1. acorn
2. table
3. paper
4. program
5. oasis
6. might
7. pint
8. even
9. pupil
10. music
11. seam
12. hotel
13. eagle
14. elbow

Unit 11

1. acorn
2. table
3. paper
4. program
5. oasis
6. might
7. pint
8. even
9. pupil
10. music
11. seam
12. hotel
13. eagle
14. elbow

A. Write the spelling words that have the long **a** sound.

1. _____ 2. _____

3. _____ 4. _____

B. Write the spelling words that have the long **e** sound.

1. _____ 2. _____

3. _____

C. Write the spelling words that have the long **o** sound.

1. _____ 2. _____

3. _____ 4. _____

D. Write the spelling words that have the long **i** sound.

1. _____ 2. _____

E. Write the spelling words that have the long **u** sound.

1. _____ 2. _____

F. Write the spelling word that has both a long **o** and a long **a**.

_____

G. Write the spelling words that are only one syllable.

1. _____ 2. _____

3. _____

A. Write a spelling word for each definition.

1. the line along which two pieces join _____
2. a fertile place in a desert _____
3. smooth or level _____
4. half a quart _____
5. a student _____
6. great force; power; strength _____

B. Write each of these words in syllables using hyphens. Use your glossary.

1. elbow _____   2. acorn _____
3. hotel _____   4. paper _____
5. eagle _____   6. even _____
7. table _____   8. music _____
9. program _____

C. Unscramble the letters to write spelling words.

1. piplu _____
2. higmt _____
3. simuc _____
4. repap _____
5. bleow _____

Fill in the blanks with spelling words to complete each story.

Our graduation was planned for April 16, 2012. Each (1) _____ would be involved (2) _____ if they were not a senior. The (3) _____ schedules were lying on a (4) _____ by the door. They were copied on special graduation (5) _____. The students sang a song with pre-recorded (6) _____. If they did not use microphones, some people (7) _____ not have been able to hear them. No one came from a long distance, so they did not have to stay in a (8) _____.

If you passed through a desert, you might see an (1) _____. There are not many trees in a desert, so you probably would not see an (2) _____ falling from a tree. You also might not see an (3) _____ flying in the sky. Because it is so hot, you may need more than a (4) _____ of water. It should not be so crowded that you would hit someone's (5) _____. Wear loose clothing so you will not tear a (6) _____ when trying to leave quickly.

Write the spelling words three times.

1. acorn _____ _____

   _____

2. table _____ _____

   _____

3. paper _____ _____

   _____

4. program_____ _____

   _____

5. oasis _____ _____

   _____

6. might _____ _____

   _____

7. pint _____ _____

   _____

8. even _____ _____

   _____

9. pupil _____ _____

   _____

10. music _____   _____

_____

11. seam _____   _____

_____

12. hotel _____   _____

_____

13. eagle _____   _____

_____

14. elbow _____   _____

_____

Unit 12
Review

Ask teacher for test.

Part 1 Grade _____

Part 2 Grade _____

Part 3 Grade _____

Part 4 Grade _____

Unit 13

This lesson has words with an **r-controlled** vowel sound.

1. bargain
2. bare
3. unfair
4. farther
5. dairy
6. merry
7. pear
8. errand
9. square
10. prepare
11. error
12. marble
13. share
14. tearing

    The **r-controlled** vowel sound you hear in **care** can be spelled using the letters **air**, **are**, **ear**, and **err**. Some words on the list have the **r-controlled** vowel sound you hear in **car**. This sound is usually spelled with the letters **ar**.

Unit 13

1. bargain
2. bare
3. unfair
4. farther
5. dairy
6. merry
7. pear

8. errand
9. square
10. prepare
11. error
12. marble
13. share
14. tearing

A. Write the spelling words that have the **ar** sound you hear in **car**.

1. _____   2. _____

3. _____

B. Write the spelling words in which the **r-controlled** vowel sound you hear in **ferry** is spelled **err**.

1. _____   2. _____

3. _____

C. Write the spelling words in which the **r-controlled** vowel sound you hear in **mare** is spelled **ear**.

1. _____   2. _____

D. Write the spelling words in which the **r-controlled** vowel sound you hear in **mare** is spelled **air**.

1. _____   2. _____

E. Write the spelling words in which the **r-controlled** vowel sound you hear in **mare** is spelled **are**.

1. _____   2. _____

3. _____   4. _____

F. Write the spelling word that is a homophone for each of these words.

1. pair _____   2. bear _____

A. Words in a dictionary which have more than one syllable have one syllable which is stressed more than the others. An accent mark (') is used to show the stresses syllable. Find each of these words in your spelling glossary. Divide them into syllables and put in the accent marks.

1. bargain _____

2. unfair _____

3. farther _____

4. dairy _____

5. errand _____

6. merry _____

7. prepare _____

8. marble _____

9. error _____

10. tearing _____

B. Write a spelling word for each of these definitions.

1. without clothing, uncluttered _____

2. a fruit _____

3. a shape with four equal sides _____

4. to use something together with someone else _____

5. mistake, something done that is wrong _____

6. a trip to get something _____

A. Complete the sentences with spelling words. You will need to add **s** to one word.

1. I like to get _____ at the thrift store.

2. Please do not make an _____ on your spelling test.

3. Can Benjamin run _____ then Byron?

4. The shredder was _____ the paper.

5. James was willing to do the _____ for me.

6. In this life we have a chance to _____ for Heaven.

7. Please _____ your toys with others.

8. In December many people say, "_____ Christmas."

9. We bought milk at Ehrler's _____.

10. In winter most trees are _____.

11. It seems so _____ for a baby to die.

B. Write a spelling word to complete each set.

1. circle, rectangle, _____

2. apple, peach, _____

3. ball, yo-yo, _____

Write the spelling words three times.

1. bargain _____ _____

   _____

2. bare _____ _____

   _____

3. unfair _____ _____

   _____

4. farther _____ _____

   _____

5. dairy _____ _____

   _____

6. merry _____ _____

   _____

7. pear _____ _____

   _____

8. errand _____ _____

   _____

9. square _____ _____

   _____

10. prepare _____ _____

_____

11. error _____ _____

_____

12. marble _____ _____

_____

13. share _____ _____

_____

14. tearing _____ _____

_____

Unit 14

This lesson has words with an **r-controlled** vowel sound.

1. rear
2. clear
3. appear
4. zero
5. shears
6. disappear
7. hero
8. period
9. cheer
10. reindeer
11. pioneer
12. year
13. jeer
14. tear

The **r-controlled** vowel sound you hear in **deer** can be spelled using the letters **eer**, **ear**, **er**, and the letter **e**.

Unit 14

1. rear
2. clear
3. appear
4. zero
5. shears
6. disappear
7. hero
8. period
9. cheer
10. reindeer
11. pioneer
12. year
13. jeer
14. tear

A. Write the spelling words that have the **ear** sound you hear in **fear** spelled with **ear**.

1. _____ 2. _____

3. _____ 4. _____

5. _____ 6. _____

7. _____

B. Write the spelling words that have the **ear** sound you hear in **fear** spelled with **eer**.

1. _____ 2. _____

3. _____ 4. _____

C. Write the spelling words that have the long **e** sound spelled with an **e**.

1. _____ 2. _____

D. Write the spelling word that has the long **e** sound spelled with **er**.

_____

E. Write the spelling word that has a prefix.

_____

F. Write the spelling word that is a compound word.

_____

A. Write the spelling word for each dictionary pronunciation.

1. (zēr′ ō) _____ 2. (ə pēr′) _____

3. (hēr′ ō) _____ 4. (yēr) _____

5. (tēr) _____ 6. (klēr) _____

7. (pī ə nēr′) _____

8. (pēr′ ē əd) _____

B. Write the word that is an antonym for each of these words.

1. front _____ 2. appear _____

C. Write a spelling word for each of these definitions.

1. the figure 0 _____

2. to make fun in a rude or unkind way _____

3. a sound of encouragement _____

4. large scissors _____

5. a kind of deer that lives in the north _____

Complete the story by using spelling words. You will need to add an **s** to two words and **ed** to one.

Daniel Boone was a famous (1) _____

during colonial times. It was a time (2) _____ in

history when there was war between the Indians and the Americans. Daniel

was born in a log cabin which probably did not have a (3) _____

door. These log cabins were heated by a fireplace when the weather was near

(4) _____. Daniel joined the military and heard

stories about Kentucky which brought him much (5) _____.

Daniel eventually was able to go to Kentucky where he was able to kill wild

animals. He might have even killed a (6) _____.

One time Daniel left his home and did not (7) _____

there again for two (8) _____. One might have

wondered if he had just (9) _____. It

was his desire to (10) _____ a path for others to

go to Kentucky. He led a group of men who did just that. They cleared the path.

The path was thick with underbrush. They needed more than

(11) _____ to clear that path, but they did it. Daniel

was such a (12) _____ that no one should ever utter a

(13) _____ against him. Some probably shed

(14) _____ at his funeral.

86

Write the spelling words three times.

1. rear _____ _____

   _____

2. clear _____ _____

   _____

3. appear _____ _____

   _____

4. zero _____ _____

   _____

5. shears _____ _____

   _____

6. disappear _____ _____

   _____

7. hero _____ _____

   _____

8. period _____ _____

   _____

9. cheer _____ _____

   _____

10. reindeer _____   _____

   _____

11. pioneer _____   _____

   _____

12. year _____   _____

   _____

13. jeer _____   _____

   _____

14. tear _____   _____

   _____

Unit 15

This lesson has words with an **r-controlled** vowel sound.

1. thorn
2. sports
3. order
4. oar
5. porch
6. important
7. storm
8. tornado
9. bored
10. course
11. short
12. fourth
13. fourteen
14. award

The **r-controlled** vowel sound you hear in **bore** can be spelled using the letters **or**, **oar**, **ar**, and **our**.

Unit 15

1. thorn
2. sports
3. order
4. oar
5. porch
6. important
7. storm
8. tornado
9. bored
10. course
11. short
12. fourth
13. fourteen
14. award

A. Write the spelling words that have the **or** sound you hear in **for** spelled with **or**.

1. _____ 2. _____

3. _____ 4. _____

5. _____ 6. _____

7. _____ 8. _____

9. _____

B. Write the spelling words that have the **or** sound you hear in **for** spelled with **our**.

1. _____ 2. _____

3. _____

C. Write the spelling word that has the **or** sound spelled with **oar**.

_____

D. Write the spelling word that has the **or** sound spelled with **ar**.

_____

E. Write the spelling words that have three syllables.

1. _____ 2. _____

F. Write the spelling words that have two syllables.

1. _____ 2. _____

3. _____

A. Find the spelling word in each sentence. Write the word and write the part of speech for each word. Use your spelling glossary if you need help.

1. I had never seen such a bad wind storm.

   _____   _____

2. Are you in the fourth grade? _____ _____

3. James enlarged the porch on our house.

   _____   _____

4. Election Day is an important day.

   _____   _____

B. Write a spelling word for each definition.

   1. the number after thirteen _____

   2. a strong whirlwind _____

   3. a command _____

   4. a direction taken _____

   5. a paddle used to row a boat _____

   6. to be uninterested _____

   7. a pointed growth on a rose bush _____

   8. a game using physical exercise _____

   9. not tall _____

   10. a prize _____

Write a spelling word to complete each sentence. You will need to add an **s** to one word.

1. The wind _____ caused us to lose our electrical power.

2. It is very _____ to read your Bible every day.

3. I received the _____ for winning the spelling bee.

4. A deck is like a big _____ on the house.

5. Byron has _____ legs like his dad.

6. Football and basketball are popular _____ in America.

7. What _____ will you take in life after graduation?

8. Roses are beautiful, but I do not like the _____ on the bush.

9. When I go to a restaurant, I like for them to fill my _____

    properly.

10. Mrs. Lewis was my _____ grade teacher.

11. The _____ did much damage to buildings, but no one

    was killed.

12. You will need more than one _____ to row a boat properly.

13. We had heard the information many times, so it was easy to get

    _____ while it was explained to the new workers.

14. I was _____ years old when Brenda got married.

Write the spelling words three times.

1. thorn

2. sports

3. order

4. oar

5. porch

6. important

7. storm

8. tornado

9. bored

10. course _____   _____

　　_____

11. short _____   _____

　　_____

12. fourth _____   _____

　　_____

13. fourteen _____   _____

　　_____

14. award _____   _____

　　_____

Unit 16

This lesson has words with an **r-controlled** vowel sound.

1. twirl
2. chirp
3. churn
4. dirty
5. journal
6. surface
7. burro
8. journey
9. worker
10. thirsty
11. further
12. search
13. church
14. learn

The **r-controlled** vowel sound you hear in **term** can be spelled using the letters **ir**, **ur**, **our**, **er**, and **ear**.

Unit 16

1. twirl
2. chirp
3. churn
4. dirty
5. journal
6. surface
7. burro
8. journey
9. worker
10. thirsty
11. further
12. search
13. church
14. learn

A. Write the spelling words that have the **er** sound you hear in **bird** spelled with **ir**.

1. _____ 2. _____

3. _____ 4. _____

B. Write the spelling words that have the **er** sound you hear in **bird** spelled with **ur**.

1. _____ 2. _____

3. _____ 4. _____

5. _____

C. Write the spelling word that has the **er** sound spelled with an **or**.

_____

D. Write the spelling words that have the **er** sound spelled with **ear**.

1. _____ 2. _____

E. Write the spelling words that have the **er** sound spelled with **our**.

1. _____ 2. _____

F. Letters have been left out of these words. Fill in the missing letters.

1. ch _____ ch   2. l _____ n   3. j _____ nal

4. tw _____ l   5. w _____ ker   6. th _____ sty

A. Write the spelling word for each dictionary pronunciation.

1. (dėr′ tē) _____

2. (jėr′ nē) _____

3. (twėrl) _____

4. (wėr′ kər) _____

5. (fėr′ thər) _____

6. (thėr′ stē) _____

7. (jėr′ nəl) _____

B. One word in each set is misspelled. Write the word correctly.

1. learn   stire   dirty _____

2. worker   twirl   charn _____

3. chirp   lern   surface _____

4. further   stir   serch _____

C. Write these words in alphabetical order.

    church   chirp   surface   burro   worker   twirl

1. _____   4. _____

2. _____   5. _____

3. _____   6. _____

Write a spelling word for each definition.

1. _____ the outside or top of something
2. _____ an effort to find something
3. _____ to spin around
4. _____ a small donkey
5. _____ to gain knowledge or skill
6. _____ a butter making container
7. _____ dry from lack of water
8. _____ not clean
9. _____ someone who works
10. _____ more
11. _____ a sound a bird makes
12. _____ a newspaper or diary
13. _____ a building for public Christian worship
14. _____ a trip

Write the spelling words three times.

1. twirl

2. chirp

3. churn

4. dirty

5. journal

6. surface

7. burro

8. journey

9. worker

10. thirsty _____ _____

11. further _____ _____

12. search _____ _____

13. church _____ _____

14. learn _____ _____

Unit 17

This lesson has words with an **r-controlled** vowel sound.

1. favor
2. color
3. gather
4. rather
5. regular
6. cannery
7. cellar
8. better
9. enter
10. collar
11. butter
12. matter
13. calendar
14. visitor

The **r-controlled** vowel sound you hear in **bird** can be spelled using the letters **or**, **er**, and **ar**.

Unit 17

1. favor
2. color
3. gather
4. rather
5. regular
6. cannery
7. cellar
8. better
9. enter
10. collar
11. butter
12. matter
13. calendar
14. visitor

A. Write the spelling words that have the **er** sound you hear in **term** spelled with **er**.

1. _____ 2. _____

3. _____ 4. _____

5. _____ 6. _____

7. _____

B. Write the spelling words that have the **er** sound spelled by the letters **ar**.

1. _____ 2. _____

3. _____ 4. _____

C. Write the spelling words that have the **er** sound spelled by the letters **or**.

1. _____ 2. _____

3. _____

D. Write the spelling words that have three syllables.

1. _____ 2. _____

3. _____ 4. _____

E. Write a spelling word that rhymes with each of these words.

1. flavor _____ 2. rather _____

3. batter _____ 4. flutter _____

A. Write the spelling word for the picture.

_____

B. Write the word for each definition.

1. _____ a place where food is put into cans

2. _____ to be important

3. _____ a kindness; something nice that you do for someone

4. _____ a person who visits

C. Write the spelling word that is an antonym for these words.

1. separate _____

2. worse   _____

3. exit   _____

D. Write these words in alphabetical order.

color   gather   butter   regular   collar   rather

1. _____   4. _____

2. _____   5. _____

3. _____   6. _____

Use your spelling words to complete the sentences.

1. Please _____ the room quietly.

2. Which _____ do you favor, blue or green?

3. I like blue _____ than red.

4. Check your _____ to see what the date it.

5. I would _____ have a blue car.

6. Is there a _____ at the door?

7. Does it _____ that I answered the phone?

8. They went to the _____ to be safe from the tornado.

9. Do you know how vegetables are canned in a _____?

10. Do you _____ corn more than green beans?

11. James's _____ was sticking up.

12. _____ all your supplies.

13. The weather last winter was not the _____

    winter weather.

14. Do you want _____ on your toast?

Write the spelling words three times.

1. favor

2. color

3. gather

4. rather

5. regular

6. cannery

7. cellar

8. better

9. enter

10. collar _____   _____

    _____

11. butter _____   _____

    _____

12. matter _____   _____

    _____

13. calendar _____   _____

    _____

14. visitor _____   _____

    _____

Unit 18
Review

Ask teacher for test.

Part 1 Grade _____

Part 2 Grade _____

Part 3 Grade _____

Part 4 Grade _____

Unit 19

Each of these words contains two letters that spell one sound.

1. knock
2. wrong
3. write
4. wrinkle
5. wreck
6. wrist
7. knob
8. knee
9. kneel
10. guess
11. guest
12. guard
13. guitar
14. guilty

The letters **kn** spell the **n** sound. The letters **wr** spell the **r** sound. The letters **gu** spell the **g** sound you hear in **goat**.

Unit 19

1. knock
2. wrong
3. write
4. wrinkle
5. wreck
6. wrist
7. knob
8. knee
9. kneel
10. guess
11. guest
12. guard
13. guitar
14. guilty

A. Write the spelling words that begin with the **kn**.

1. _____ 2. _____

3. _____ 4. _____

B. Write the spelling words that have the **wr**.

1. _____ 2. _____

3. _____ 4. _____

5. _____

C. Write the spelling words that begin with the **gu**.

1. _____ 2. _____

3. _____ 4. _____

5. _____

D. Write the spelling word that rhymes with each of these words.

1. sock _____ 2. bite _____

3. best _____ 4. hard _____

5. seal _____ 6. long _____

E. Write the spelling words that have two syllables.

1. _____ 2. _____

3. _____

A. Guide words are the two words printed at the top of a dictionary page. The guide word at the top left is the first entry word on that page. The guide word at the top right is the last entry word on that page. The words in between are written in alphabetical order. Write the spelling word or words that would be on the same page as the guide words.

1. **knead - knife** _____ _____

2. **knit - knuckle** _____ _____

3. **wring - written** _____ _____

   _____

4. **grunt - guide** _____ _____

   _____

B. One word in each set is misspelled. Write the word correctly.

1. wrong, wreck, guiltey _____

2. guiter, guard, wrong _____

3. wreck, rong, wrinkle _____

4. knobe, knock, kneel _____

C. Write the spelling word that is an antonym of each word.

1. innocent _____   2. right _____

D. Write these words in syllables using hyphens between the syllables. Use your spelling glossary if you need help.

   1. guilty _____   2. guitar _____

A. Use spelling words to complete the story.

I would like to learn to play the (1) _____. I could hold the guitar on one (2) _____. I might even (3) _____ my own songs. While learning to play, I would probably touch the (4) _____ string sometimes. I should (5) _____ against hurting my right (6) _____. That might (7) _____ me out of playing. I (8) _____ I should practice daily to keep from making a mistake and feeling (9) _____ in front of\ a (10) _____.

B. Use the code to make spelling words.

b = 1	c = 2	e = 3	i = 4	k = 5
l = 6	n = 7	o = 8	r = 9	w = 10

1. 10 + 9 + 3 + 2 + 5 = _____

2. 5 + 7 + 3 + 3 + 6 = _____

3. 10 + 9 + 4 + 7 + 5 + 6 + 3 = _____

4. 5 + 7 + 8 + 1 = _____

Write the spelling words three times.

1. knock _____ _____
   _____

2. wrong _____ _____
   _____

3. write _____ _____
   _____

4. wrinkle _____ _____
   _____

5. wreck _____ _____
   _____

6. wrist _____ _____
   _____

7. knob _____ _____
   _____

8. knee _____ _____
   _____

9. kneel _____ _____
   _____

10. guess _____   _____

_____

11. guest _____   _____

_____

12. guard _____   _____

_____

13. guitar _____   _____

_____

14. guilty _____   _____

_____

Unit 20

These words have a silent letter in them.

1. aunt
2. bought
3. thumb
4. build
5. lamb
6. often
7. castle
8. soften
9. honor
10. whistle
11. sign
12. crumb
13. listen
14. comb

Each of these words have a silent letter in it. For example the **u** is not heard in the word **aunt**.

Unit 20

1. aunt
2. bought
3. thumb
4. build
5. lamb
6. often
7. castle
8. soften
9. honor
10. whistle
11. sign
12. crumb
13. listen
14. comb

A. Write the spelling words that contain a silent **b**.

1. _____   2. _____

3. _____   4. _____

B. Write the spelling words that contain a silent **g**.

1. _____   2. _____

C. Write the spelling words that contain a silent **t**.

1. _____   2. _____

3. _____   4. _____

5. _____

D. Write the spelling words that contain a silent **u**.

1. _____   2. _____

3. _____

E. Write the spelling words that have a silent **h**.

1. _____   2. _____

F. Write the spelling word that rhymes with each of these words.

1. ant _____   2. thought _____

3. mine _____   4. roam _____

A. Write the spelling word for each dictionary pronunciation.

1. (bĭld) _____ 2. (krŭm) _____

3. (ănt) _____ 4. (kōm) _____

5. (kăs′ əl) _____ 6. (thŭm) _____

7. (hwĭs′ əl) _____ 8. (ô′ fən) _____

9. (lăm) _____ 10. (sôf′ ən) _____

11. (sīn) _____ 12. (bôt) _____

13. (ŏn′ ər) _____ 14. (lĭs′ ən) _____

B. Write each of these spelling words in syllables. Put hyphens between the syllables.

1. often _____

2. castle _____

3. soften _____

4. honor _____

5. whistle _____

6. listen _____

C. Write a spelling word for each definition.

1. _____ the wife of an uncle

2. _____ a baby sheep

3. _____ the home of a king or queen

A. Write a spelling word to complete each sentence.

1. We have one _____ on each hand.

2. My _____ Mae was one hundred years old on July 31, 2012.

3. We should wash our hands _____ to prevent sickness.

4. I love for someone to _____ my hair.

5. Even though there is no king in Lexington, there was a _____ built there.

6. Can you read the _____?

7. We should _____ our parents.

8. Do not leave a _____ of food on the floor.

9. I could hear Mark _____ for his dog.

B. Write a spelling word to complete each comparison.

1. sell is to buy as sold is to _____

2. hot is to cold as harden is to _____

3. black is to white as ignore is to _____

4. cow is to calf as sheep is to _____

5. right is to left as destroy is to _____

Write the spelling words three times.

1. aunt

2. bought

3. thumb

4. build

5. lamb

6. often

7. castle

8. soften

9. honor

10. whistle _____   _____

_____

11. sign _____   _____

_____

12. crumb _____   _____

_____

13. listen _____   _____

_____

14. comb _____   _____

_____

Unit 21

In the English language, the letter **q** is usually followed by the letter **u**. These two letters together make the **kw** sound.

1. queen
2. quietness
3. quarter
4. question
5. quarrel
6. quick
7. quitter

8. squirrel
9. squirm
10. squash
11. squeal
12. squeeze
13. squeak
14. squaw

Unit 21

1. queen
2. quietness
3. quarter
4. question
5. quarrel
6. quick
7. quitter
8. squirrel
9. squirm
10. squash
11. squeal
12. squeeze
13. squeak
14. squaw

A. Write the spelling words that begin with the first sound of **square**.

1. _____ 2. _____

3. _____ 4. _____

5. _____ 6. _____

7. _____

B. Write the spelling words that begin with the first sound of **quiz**..

1. _____ 2. _____

3. _____ 4. _____

5. _____ 6. _____

7. _____

C. Write the spelling words that have two syllables.

1. _____ 2. _____

3. _____ 4. _____

5. _____

D. Write the spelling word that has three syllables.

_____

E. Write the spelling words that fit these definitions.

1. twenty-five cents _____

2. very fast _____

A. Write these words in alphabetical order.

queen   quarter   question   quietness   quarrel

1. _____   4. _____

2. _____   5. _____

3. _____

B. Write these words in alphabetical order.

squirrel   squash   squirm   squeal   squaw

1. _____   4. _____

2. _____   5. _____

3. _____

C. One word in each set is misspelled. Write the word correctly.

1. quik, squeeze, squirm _____

2. squaw, question, quiter _____

3. squeze, queen, quarter _____

4. quietness, quarrel, squeek _____

D. Write these words in syllables using hyphens between the syllables. Use your spelling glossary if you need help.

1. quietness _____   2. quarter _____

3. question _____   4. quarrel _____

5. squirrel _____

Write a spelling word to complete each sentence.

1. I like to eat baked _____.

2. _____ Victoria lived long ago in England.

3. A _____ is an animal that likes to climb trees.

4. It is not good to _____ with others.

5. If you have a _____, raise your hand.

6. Do not _____ an orange too hard if you do not want juice on your hand.

7. Was Pocahontas an Indian _____?

8. Benjamin would _____ with delight.

9. He also likes to _____ instead of sit still.

10. I am not a _____ learner.

11. Please enter the room with _____ if someone is taking a test.

12. Two dimes and one nickel equal one _____.

13. I do not like to hear a chair _____.

14. You will not accomplish much in life if you are a _____.

Write the spelling words three times.

1. queen _____ _____

  _____

2. quietness _____ _____

  _____

3. quarter _____ _____

  _____

4. question _____ _____

  _____

5. quarrel _____ _____

  _____

6. quick _____ _____

  _____

7. quitter _____ _____

  _____

8. squirrel _____ _____

  _____

9. squirm _____ _____

  _____

10. squash

11. squeal

12. squeeze

13. squeak

14. squaw

Unit 22

The spelling words in this lesson begin with the consonant clusters **scr** and **str**.

1. strange
2. strain
3. strap
4. scrap
5. scratch
6. scrub
7. stream
8. straight
9. string
10. scream
11. screen
12. strike
13. strong
14. scrapbook

A **consonant cluster** is a group of letters. The sounds of the letters blend together so closely that they seem to make one sound, but the sound of each letter can still be heard.

Unit 22

1. strange
2. strain
3. strap
4. scrap
5. scratch
6. scrub
7. stream
8. straight
9. string
10. scream
11. screen
12. strike
13. strong
14. scrapbook

A. Write the spelling words that begin with the consonant cluster **str**.

1. _____ 2. _____

3. _____ 4. _____

5. _____ 6. _____

7. _____ 8. _____

B. Write the spelling words that begin with the consonant cluster **scr**.

1. _____ 2. _____

3. _____ 4. _____

5. _____ 6. _____

C. Write the spelling word or words that rhyme with each of these words.

1. pain _____

2. eight _____

3. dream _____

4. range _____

D. Write the spelling word that is a compound word.

_____

E. Write the spelling word for each definition.

1. great strength _____

2. unusual _____

A. Write the spelling words in each set in alphabetical order.

strange   string   stream

1. _____   3. _____

2. _____

screen   scrap   scrub

1. _____   3. _____

2. _____

strap   strain   straight

1. _____   3. _____

2. _____

B. One word in each set is misspelled. Write the word correctly.

1. screen, scrach, strange _____

2. screem, strap, straight _____

3. strain, striek, stream _____

C. Write the spelling words that fit these definitions.

1. a book to keep pictures or newspaper clippings in

    _____

2. not crooked _____

Write a spelling word to complete each sentence.

1. It does not make a pleasant sound to _____ on a chalkboard with your fingernails.

2. It is best to have a _____ on a window to keep bugs from coming into the house.

3. James had a _____ dream.

4. Use a ruler to keep your lines _____.

5. Did you put pictures into a _____?

6. Which wall did you _____ with a brush?

7. I was using _____ paper to work the math problems.

8. Did Clarence put the shoulder _____ on Ben?

9. It would make me wonder what was happening if I heard a woman _____.

10. Lifting a piano can _____ your back.

11. It takes a _____ person to lift a piano.

12. I tried to _____ a match on the box.

13. There was more than a _____ running across our yard after all the rain.

14. Get some _____ to put onto your kite.

Write the spelling words three times.

1. strange

2. strain

3. strap

4. scrap

5. scratch

6. scrub

7. stream

8. straight

9. string

10. scream _____   _____

   _____

11. screen _____   _____

   _____

12. strike _____   _____

   _____

13. strong _____   _____

   _____

14. scrapbook _____

   _____

   _____

Unit 23

The spelling words in this lesson end with the consonant clusters **ld, nd,** or **nk**.

1. scold
2. field
3. mind
4. mound
5. wink
6. blink
7. ink
8. wild
9. bald
10. blind
11. grind
12. sank
13. blank
14. blend

A **consonant cluster** can appear at the beginning or ending of words. The consonant clusters appear at the end of these words.

Unit 23

1. scold
2. field
3. mind
4. mound
5. wink
6. blink
7. ink

8. wild
9. bald
10. blind
11. grind
12. sank
13. blank
14. blend

A. Write the spelling words that end with the consonant cluster **ld**.

1. _____   2. _____

3. _____   4. _____

B. Write the spelling words that begin with the consonant cluster **nd**.

1. _____   2. _____

3. _____   4. _____

5. _____

C. Write the spelling words that begin with the consonant cluster **nk**.

1. _____   2. _____

3. _____   4. _____

5. _____

D. Write the spelling words that begin and end with a consonant cluster.

1. _____   2. _____

3. _____   4. _____

5. _____   6. _____

E. Write the spelling word that has the word **old** in it.

_____

F. Write the spelling words that have the word **ink** in them.

1. _____   2. _____

A. Write a spelling word for each definition.

   1. a small hill; pile of earth _____

   2. a colored liquid used for writing _____

   3. to find fault with someone _____

   4. to wink very fast _____

   5. having no hair _____

   6. an empty space on a paper _____

   7. not tamed _____

B. One word in each set is misspelled. Write the word correctly.

1. scold, feild, ink _____

2. miend, mound, blank _____

3. wenk, bald, blink _____

4. field, griend, wild _____

5. mind, wink, sangk _____

C. Write the spelling words that fit these definitions.

   1. not being able to see _____

   2. to mix together _____

A. Write a spelling word to complete the story.

You would not want to choose a (1) _____ person to play on a baseball team. You would want a person with a good aim to stand on the pitcher's (2) _____. If you are standing on the (3) _____, and a ball is coming toward you, you need to have your (4) _____ on what you are doing and don't (5) _____ an eye.

If another player misses the ball, do not (6) _____ them. They may be doing their best. If someone hits a home run, the crowd may sound as if they have gone (7) _____.

B. Write a spelling word to complete each sentence.

1. The Titanic _____ to the bottom of the ocean.

2. You can _____ with one eye.

3. I like to write with an _____ pen.

4. William did not like the fact that his head was almost _____.

5. Do not leave any spaces _____.

6. _____ the eggs, oil, water, and brownie mix with a spoon.

7. _____ some nuts and put them into the mixture.

Write the spelling words three times.

1. scold _____   _____

   _____

2. field _____   _____

   _____

3. mind _____   _____

   _____

4. mound _____   _____

   _____

5. wink _____   _____

   _____

6. blink _____   _____

   _____

7. ink _____   _____

   _____

8. wild _____   _____

   _____

9. bald _____   _____

   _____

10. blind   _____   _____

    _____

11. grind   _____   _____

    _____

12. sank   _____   _____

    _____

13. blank   _____   _____

    _____

14. blend   _____   _____

    _____

Unit 24
Review

Ask teacher for test.

Part 1 Grade _____

Part 2 Grade _____

Part 3 Grade _____

Part 4 Grade _____

Unit 25

The spelling words in this lesson are singular and plural nouns.

1. life
2. calf
3. knife
4. goose
5. tooth
6. woman
7. child

8. lives
9. calves
10. knives
11. geese
12. teeth
13. women
14. children

To make nouns that end if **f** or **fe** plural, usually change the **f** or **fe** to **v** and add **es**.

Some nouns form their plural form by changing the word such as the word **child** changes to **children** for the plural form.

Unit 25

1. life
2. calf
3. knife
4. goose
5. tooth
6. woman
7. child

8. lives
9. calves
10. knives
11. geese
12. teeth
13. women
14. children

A. Write the plural form of each of these spelling words.

1. life _____

2. calf _____

3. knife _____

B. Write the plural form of each of these spelling words.

1. goose _____

2. tooth _____

3. woman _____

4. child _____

C. Write the spelling words that have double vowels.

1. _____ 2. _____

3. _____ 4. _____

D. Write the spelling words whose first letter is silent.

1. _____ 2. _____

E. Write the spelling word that is the base word for each of these words.

1. calves _____

2. lives _____

3. knives _____

A. Write the spelling word for each dictionary pronunciation.

1. (kăf) _____ 2. (gēs) _____

3. (līvz) _____ 4. (wum′ ən) _____

5. (nīvz) _____ 6. (tüth) _____

B. Write a spelling word for each definition.

1. _____ young cows

2. _____ a flying creature

3. _____ a cutting utensil

4. _____ things used to chew food

5. _____ a young person

6. _____ something we only have one of

C. Write each of these spelling words in syllables. Put hyphens between the syllables.

1. women _____

2. children _____

D. Use the code to find the spelling words.

e = 1   f = 2   i = 3   k = 4   l = 5   n = 6   s = 7   v = 8

1. 5 + 3 + 2 + 1 = _____

2. 5 + 3 + 8 + 1 + 7 = _____

3. 4 + 6 + 3 + 2 + 1 _____

4. 4 + 6 + 3 + 8 + 1 + 7 _____

Write a spelling word to complete each sentence. The first letter has been given.

1. Some w_____want jobs that pay as much as men's jobs.

2. A nursing job is a high paying job for a w_____.

3. Donna got her first t_____when she was five months old.

4. All of James's t_____are false.

5. I knew Clarence had one k_____.

6. I did not know he had more than ten k_____.

7. Jennifer has one c_____.

8. Donna has four c_____.

9. Every g_____should be able to fly.

10. Many g_____fly south.

11. Abraham Lincoln went to see a play and lost his l_____.

12. Many l_____were lost in the Civil War.

13. I have never seen a c_____being born.

14. Not many cows have two c_____at one time.

Write the spelling words three times.

1. life

2. calf

3. knife

4. goose

5. tooth

6. woman

7. child

8. lives

9. calves

10. knives   _____   _____

            _____

11. geese   _____   _____

            _____

12. teeth   _____   _____

            _____

13. women   _____   _____

            _____

14. children _____   _____

            _____

Unit 26

The spelling words in this lesson are plural nouns.

1. beauties
2. ponies
3. pennies
4. valleys
5. babies
6. donkeys
7. funnies
8. monkeys
9. delays
10. days
11. toys
12. stories
13. libraries
14. trays

Base words ending with a **vowel** and a **y** are made plural by adding an **s**. Base words ending with a **consonant** and a **y** are made plural by changing the **y** to **i** and adding **es**.

Unit 26

1. beauties
2. ponies
3. pennies
4. valleys
5. babies
6. donkeys
7. funnies
8. monkeys
9. delays
10. days
11. toys
12. stories
13. libraries
14. trays

A. Write the spelling words that are formed by changing the final **y** of the base word to an **i** before adding the **es**.

1. _____ 2. _____

3. _____ 4. _____

5. _____ 6. _____

7. _____

B. Write the spelling words that are formed by only adding **s** to the base word.

1. _____ 2. _____

3. _____ 4. _____

5. _____ 6. _____

7. _____

C. Write the plural form of each of these words.

1. story _____

2. beauty _____

3. library _____

4. baby _____

5. donkey _____

D. Write the spelling word that rhymes with each of these words.

1. boys _____ 2. bunnies _____

A. Pretend the boldfaced words are guide words. Write the spelling words that would come between them in the dictionary.

1. **pane - pine** _____

2. **dad - deck** _____

3. **fume - fur** _____

4. **pine - postage** _____

B. One word in each pair is misspelled. Write the word that is spelled correctly.

1. valleys, vallies _____

2. toyes, toys _____

3. babys, babies _____

4. beauties, beautys _____

5. trays, traies _____

C. Write these words in syllables using hyphens between the syllables. Use your spelling glossary if you need help.

1. donkeys _____

2. monkeys _____

3. stories _____

4. delays _____

5. libraries _____

Write a spelling word to complete each sentence.

1. How many _____ of school are left?

2. We went to two different _____ to find the movie of Mt. Rushmore.

3. Some people like to read the _____ in the newspaper.

4. The book had thirty _____ in it.

5. Many _____ were in the zoo.

6. One hundred _____ equal one dollar.

7. Most children in America want _____ for Christmas.

8. How many _____ were in the Miss America contest?

9. Make sure everyone keeps their food on their _____.

10. There were two _____ in the field.

11. I took care of two _____ at one time in the nursery.

12. How many _____ are you willing to tolerate if you fly across the country?

13. We went into many _____ while we traveled.

14. The Bible talks about people traveling on _____.

Write the spelling words three times.

1. beauties

2. ponies

3. pennies

4. valleys

5. babies

6. donkeys

7. funnies

8. monkeys

9. delays

10. days _____   _____

_____

11. toys _____   _____

_____

12. stories _____   _____

_____

13. libraries _____   _____

_____

14. trays _____   _____

_____

Unit 27

The spelling words in this lesson have suffixes.

1. copied
2. stayed
3. replied
4. carried
5. played
6. enjoyed
7. married
8. copying
9. staying
10. replying
11. carrying
12. playing
13. enjoying
14. marrying

    Look at the spelling words that have an **ed** suffix. To form these words, first look at the letter that comes before the **y** in the base word. If the base word ends with a **vowel** and a **y**, just add **ed**. If the base word ends with a **consonant** and a **y**, change the **y** to **i** before adding the suffix **ed**.

    To form the spelling words ending in **ing**, just add the **ing** after the word. Nothing has to be changed to the base word.

Unit 27

1. copied
2. stayed
3. replied
4. carried
5. played
6. enjoyed
7. married

8. copying
9. staying
10. replying
11. carrying
12. playing
13. enjoying
14. marrying

A. Write the spelling words that are formed by changing the final **y** of the base word to an **i** before adding the **ed**.

1. _____ 2. _____

3. _____ 4. _____

B. Write the spelling words that are formed by adding **ing** to the base word.

1. _____ 2. _____

3. _____ 4. _____

5. _____ 6. _____

7. _____

C. Write the base word for each of these words.

1. stayed _____

2. playing _____

3. enjoyed _____

4. played _____

5. carried _____

6. replied _____

D. Write the spelling words that have double consonants.

1. _____ 2. _____

3. _____ 4. _____

A. Write these spelling words in syllables. Put hyphens between the syllables. Use your spelling glossary if you need help.

1. copied _____

2. copying _____

3. replying _____

4. married _____

5. replied _____

6. carrying _____

7. enjoying _____

8. marrying _____

9. carried _____

B. Write a spelling word that fits each definition.

1. remained _____

2. participating in a game _____

3. had a good time _____

C. Write these words in alphabetical order.

copied   replied   carried   married

1. _____ 3. _____

2. _____ 4. _____

Use spelling words to complete the story.

If you think you might get (1) _____ some day, you need to know there will be much work to be done to plan the wedding. First of all you need to decide who you will be(2) _____. You will want to know how many people you plan to invite so you will know how many invitations need to be (3) _____. You will not want to do all the work, so you will need to decide who will be (4) _____ these invitations for you. You may want people to send you a reply so you will know how many are coming. Then have someone count how many people (5) _____ to your invitations. If guests are coming in from another town, you may want to know how many are going to be (6) _____ in hotels. Some family members may cook the food for the reception, so there will be food (7) _____ in. They may need help (8) _____ all of it. You will also want to decide who will be (9) _____ music for your wedding. Will you have slow music or fast music (10) _____? You will want to have in your memory that everyone was (11) _____ your wedding and most of all you (12) _____ it.

Write the spelling words three times.

1. copied

2. stayed

3. replied

4. carried

5. played

6. enjoyed

7. married

8. copying

9. staying

10. replying

11. carrying

12. playing

13. enjoying

14. marrying

Unit 28

The spelling words in this lesson have suffixes.

1. shaped
2. chased
3. raced
4. decided
5. noticed
6. forced
7. creased

8. shaping
9. chasing
10. racing
11. deciding
12. noticing
13. forcing
14. creasing

Many words end with a silent **e**. That **e** is usually dropped before adding a suffix that begins with a **vowel** such as **ed** or **ing**.

Unit 28

1. shaped
2. chased
3. raced
4. decided
5. noticed
6. forced
7. creased

8. shaping
9. chasing
10. racing
11. deciding
12. noticing
13. forcing
14. creasing

A. Write the spelling words that have the long **a** sound.

1. _____ 2. _____

3. _____ 4. _____

5. _____ 6. _____

B. Write the word with the correct ending for each column.

                  ing ending   **ed** ending

1. decide _____ _____

2. notice _____ _____

3. force _____ _____

4. crease _____ _____

C. Write the spelling words that have the word **not** in them.

1. _____ 2. _____

D. Write the spelling words that have a **c** sounded with its soft sound in them.

1. _____ 2. _____

3. _____ 4. _____

5. _____ 6. _____

7. _____ 8. _____

A. Write the spelling word for each dictionary pronunciation.

1. (shāpt) _____

2. (rās′ ing) _____

3. (krēst) _____

4. (fōrst) _____

5. (dĭ sīd′ ing) _____

6. (nō′ tĭst) _____

7. (chās′ ing) _____

B. One word in each set is misspelled. Write the word correctly.

1. creasing, notising, chasing _____

2. chazed, shaped, racing _____

3. forced, shapeing, deciding _____

4. noticed, creased, decideed _____

5. chased, forceing, noticing _____

6. raceed, shaping, forced _____

7. noticing, decided, creaseing _____

C. Write the words that fit the definition.

1. _____ trying to make up your mind

2. _____ making a line by folding

Write spelling words to complete the sentences.

1. The boys _____ across the parking lot.

2. It was dangerous to be _____ when a car was backing out of a parking spot.

3. I _____ Frankie had gotten a haircut.

4. I folded the letter and _____ it.

5. I wanted the cake to be _____ like a heart.

6. I do not like to be _____ a dog, and I do not want to be _____ by one.

7. I _____ to practice on the piano.

8. No one was _____ me to learn to play.

9. You can be _____ clay figures while I'm talking.

10. Who will be _____ what kind of car we will get?

11. David was _____ the paper to make the shape of a boat.

12. We should not have to be _____ to go to church.

13. Have you been _____ that Kevin is losing weight?

Write the spelling words three times.

1. shaped
2. chased
3. raced
4. decided
5. noticed
6. forced
7. creased
8. shaping
9. chasing

10. racing   _____   _____

   _____

11. deciding _____   _____

   _____

12. noticing _____   _____

   _____

13. forcing _____   _____

   _____

14. creasing _____   _____

   _____

Unit 29

The spelling words in this lesson have suffixes.

1. larger
2. braver
3. bigger
4. madder
5. finer
6. fatter
7. nicer

8. largest
9. bravest
10. biggest
11. maddest
12. finest
13. fattest
14. nicest

These words have the **er** and **est** suffixes. The words ending in **er** can be used to compare two people or things. The words ending in **est** can be used to compare more than two people or things.

Some of the base words for these words end with a silent **e**. That **e** is dropped before adding the **er** or **est** suffix.

Other base words end with a consonant letter. The consonant is **doubled** before the suffix is added.

Unit 29

1. larger
2. braver
3. bigger
4. madder
5. finer
6. fatter
7. nicer

8. largest
9. bravest
10. biggest
11. maddest
12. finest
13. fattest
14. nicest

A. Write the spelling words that have the long **a** sound.

1. _____ 2. _____

B. Write the word with the correct ending for each base word. You will need to drop the **e** before adding the suffix.

        er ending   **est** ending

1. large _____ _____

2. fine _____ _____

3. nice _____ _____

C. Write the word with the correct ending for each base word. You will need to double the final consonant before adding the suffix.

        er ending   **est** ending

1. big _____ _____

2. mad _____ _____

3. fat _____ _____

D. Write the spelling words that have a **short a** sound in them.

1. _____ 2. _____

3. _____ 4. _____

E. Write the spelling words that have the soft sound of **c**.

1. _____ 2. _____

A. Write these spelling words in syllables. Put hyphens between the syllables. Use your spelling glossary if you need help.

1. larger _____
2. braver _____
3. bigger _____
4. madder _____
5. finer _____
6. fatter _____
7. nicer _____

B. Write these words in alphabetical order.

nicest   **biggest**   **largest**   **finest**

bravest   **maddest**   **fattest**

1. _____
2. _____
3. _____
4. _____
5. _____
6. _____
7. _____

Write spelling words to complete the sentences. The first letter of each word is given.

Dustin was (1) l_____ than Andy. He was the

(2) l_____ boy I have taught.

Leslie was (3) n_____ than some teachers, but

Mrs. Thompson was the (4) n_____.

David was willing to fight the giant. He was (5) b_____

than his brothers. He was the (6) b_____ boy

in Israel.

Haman was a wicked man. He did not like Mordecai. He wanted to have

him hanged. Queen Esther did not like what Haman wanted to do. Haman

was (7) m_____ than Queen Esther. The king was the

(8) m_____ of all of them.

Saul was (9) b_____ than David, but Goliath was the

(10) b_____ of all of them.

Was Vickie (11) f_____ than James? I believe she is the

(12) f_____ person in church.

Donna's dark blue van was (13) f_____ than the truck.

The red van was the (14) f_____ of all of them.

Write the spelling words three times.

1. larger

2. braver

3. bigger

4. madder

5. finer

6. fatter

7. nicer

8. largest _____   _____

   _____

9. bravest _____   _____

   _____

10. biggest _____   _____

    _____

11. maddest _____   _____

    _____

12. finest _____   _____

    _____

13. fattest _____   _____

    _____

14. nicest _____   _____

    _____

Unit 30
Review

Ask teacher for test.

Part 1 Grade _____

Part 2 Grade _____

Part 3 Grade _____

Part 4 Grade _____

Unit 31
These spelling words are contractions.

1. they'd
2. what's
3. we'll
4. you'd
5. who'd
6. doesn't
7. how'd
8. who's
9. he'd
10. they'll
11. I'd
12. she'd
13. aren't
14. she'll

A **contraction** is a shortened form of two words in which some letters are left out. An **apostrophe** (') is used in place of the letters that have been left out.

Some contractions are made by joining a word with **would**. All the letters of **would** are left out except **d**. The 'd can also stand for **did** or **had**.

Other contractions are made with the words **is** or **will**. For example, **what's** is the contraction for **what is**. **What's** can also mean **what has**. **We'll** is the contraction for **we will**.

Unit 31

1. they'd
2. what's
3. we'll
4. you'd
5. who'd
6. doesn't
7. how'd
8. who's
9. he'd
10. they'll
11. I'd
12. she'd
13. aren't
14. she'll

A. Write spelling words that are contractions for these words.

1. they would _____
2. you had _____
3. who had _____
4. he would _____
5. I would _____
6. she had _____
7. how did _____

B. Write the contractions formed with the word **will**.

1. _____
2. _____
3. _____

C. Write the contractions formed with the word **not**.

1. _____
2. _____

D. Write the contractions formed with the word **is**.

1. _____
2. _____

A. Write the spelling word for each dictionary pronunciation.

1. (hwŏts) _____

2. (shēd) _____

3. (houd) _____

4. (shēl) _____

5. (wēl) _____

6. (thāl) _____

7. (hüd) _____

8. (thād) _____

9. (hēd) _____

10. (ūd) _____

11. (dŭz′ ənt) _____

12. (hüz) _____

13. (īd) _____

14. (ärnt) _____

B. Write the contraction for these words.

1. who did _____ 2. how did _____

3. they would _____ 4. does not _____

5. she would _____

Use spelling words to complete the pretend conversation. The first letter of each word has been given.

Vickie: "(1) W_____ like to go to Strawberry Plains, Tennessee?"

Ola: "(2) W_____ planning to go?"

Vickie: "(3) I_____ like to go next year."

Ola: What is there to do in Tennessee?

Vickie: "(4) Y_____ maybe go to church. We (5) a_____ planning to go right now."

Ola: "Now (6) w_____ so fantastic about it?"

Vickie: "There's a church there that has very enjoyable services. If Missie and Jerry would go, I believe (7) t_____ enjoy it. Maybe (8) w_____ talk them into going with us.

Ola: "(9) D_____ Matthew have time for a vacation? (10) H_____ like it too."

Vickie: "Kayla could also go. I believe (11) s_____ enjoy it. Maybe (12) s_____ be willing to go if we get a nice motel room. I'd say (13) t_____ all be glad they went." (14) H_____ you like to go with us?

187

1. they'd _____   _____

2. what's _____   _____

3. we'll _____   _____

4. you'd _____   _____

5. who'd _____   _____

6. doesn't _____   _____

7. how'd _____   _____

8. who's _____   _____

9. he'd _____   _____

10. they'll _____   _____

_____

11. I'd _____   _____

_____

12. she'd _____   _____

_____

13. aren't _____   _____

_____

14. she'll _____   _____

_____

Unit 32

These spelling words are homophones.

1. sail
2. beat
3. tale
4. wood
5. horse
6. some
7. male

8. sale
9. beet
10. tail
11. would
12. hoarse
13. sum
14. mail

Homophones are words that sound the same, but have different meanings and spellings. You should memorize the meaning and spelling of each homophone.

Unit 32

1. sail
2. beat
3. tale
4. wood
5. horse
6. some
7. male

8. sale
9. beet
10. tail
11. would
12. hoarse
13. sum
14. mail

A. Write spelling words that are homophone for these words.

1. sale _____

2. male _____

3. would _____

4. some _____

5. hoarse _____

6. tale _____

7. beat _____

B. Write the spelling words that have the long **a** spelled with the **a** + **consonant** + **e** pattern.

1. _____ 2. _____

3. _____

C. Write the spelling word for each picture.

1. _____

2. _____

A. Write the spelling word that fits each definition.

1. _____ the answer for an addition problem

2. _____ a boy or a man

3. _____ a piece of cloth on a boat that catches the wind to move the boat

4. _____ letters or cards to be sent to someone

5. _____ a false story

6. _____ a four-legged animal with hoofs and a flowing mane

7. _____ to mix rapidly

8. _____ having a rough voice

9. _____ a white or purple vegetable

B. Write these words in alphabetical order.

| wood | some | tail | sale | would |

1. _____   4. _____

2. _____   5. _____

3. _____

C. Find these words in your spelling glossary and write the part of speech for each of them.

1. hoarse _____ 2. would _____

3. some _____   4. tail _____

Use spelling words to complete the sentences.

1. _____ you please help me add these numbers together so I can find the _____.

2. It would be nice to receive _____ chocolate chip cookies in the _____.

3. James was sick, and his voice was _____.

4. Freddy owned a _____ that would swish its _____.

5. My uncle went on the lake with his _____ boat.

6. Donna burns _____ to heat her house.

7. The piano was advertised for _____.

8. I do not want to read a _____ to children.

9. James did not grow one _____ in his garden.

10. Patti has one _____ child and one female.

11. Do not _____ the cake mix too much.

194

Write the spelling words three times.

1. sail

2. beat

3. tale

4. wood

5. horse

6. some

7. male

8. sale

9. beet

10. tail   _____   _____

    _____

11. would   _____   _____

    _____

12. hoarse _____   _____

    _____

13. sum   _____   _____

    _____

14. mail   _____   _____

    _____

Unit 33

These spelling words contain the **f** sound. The letters **ph** and **gh** are used to make the **f** sound in these words.

1. telephone
2. cough
3. dolphin
4. photo
5. tough
6. rough
7. laugh
8. phonics
9. nephew
10. orphan
11. enough
12. paragraph
13. phrase
14. pamphlet

Unit 33

1. telephone
2. cough
3. dolphin
4. photo
5. tough
6. rough
7. laugh
8. phonics
9. nephew
10. orphan
11. enough
12. paragraph
13. phrase
14. pamphlet

A. Write the spelling words that have the **f** sound spelled with a **ph**.

1. _____ 2. _____

3. _____ 4. _____

5. _____ 6. _____

7. _____ 8. _____

9. _____

B. Write the spelling words that have the **f** sound spelled with a **gh**.

1. _____ 2. _____

3. _____ 4. _____

5. _____

C. Write the spelling words that have two syllables.

1. _____ 2. _____

3. _____ 4. _____

5. _____ 6. _____

7. _____

D. Write the spelling words that have three syllables.

1. _____ 2. _____

A. Write the words for the dictionary pronunciation.

1. (tĕl′ ə fōn) _____

2. (tŭf) _____

3. (frāz) _____

4. (kôf) _____

5. (lăf) _____

6. (rŭf) _____

B. Write the word that fits each definition.

1. _____ a picture made with a camera

2. _____ a method for teaching a person to read

3. _____ a child whose parents are dead

4. _____ as many as needed

5. _____ a small whale that looks like a porpoise

6. _____ a group of sentences which belong together

7. _____ son of one's brother or sister

8. _____ a booklet in paper covers

C. Find each word in your glossary. Write its part of speech.

1. rough _____ 2. laugh _____

3. orphan _____ 4. telephone _____

A. Write a spelling word that is an antonym for each word.

1. smooth _____

2. niece _____

3. cry _____

4. easy _____

B. Complete the sentences with spelling words.

1. The woman called me on the _____.

2. I read the _____ about the illness.

3. Will you write a _____ about what has happened to you this morning?

4. Since Pasha's parents died, he was an _____.

5. Put your hand over your mouth when you _____.

6. Do you have a _____ of you when you were a baby?

7. Many people can learn to read by using _____.

8. Do you have _____ money to buy a new car?

9. A _____ is part of a sentence.

10. A _____ looks like a porpoise.

Write the spelling words three times.

1. telephone _____   _____

2. cough   _____   _____

3. dolphin   _____   _____

4. photo   _____   _____

5. tough   _____   _____

6. rough   _____   _____

7. laugh   _____   _____

8. phonics   _____   _____

9. nephew   _____   _____

10. orphan

11. enough

12. paragraph

13. phrase

14. pamphlet

Unit 34

These spelling words contain suffixes.

1. enjoyable
2. disturbance
3. shortage
4. baggage
5. passage
6. available
7. postage
8. acceptable
9. insurance
10. assistance
11. wooden
12. sadden
13. tiresome
14. wholesome

Suffixes can change the meaning of a word. The suffix **able** means "*capable of.*" The suffix **ance** means "*quality or state of.*" The suffix **age** means "*collection of.*" The suffix **en** means "*made of.*" The suffix **some** means "*quality, state, or action.*"

Unit 34

1. enjoyable
2. disturbance
3. shortage
4. baggage
5. passage
6. available
7. postage
8. acceptable
9. insurance
10. assistance
11. wooden
12. sadden
13. tiresome
14. wholesome

A. Write the spelling words that have the **able** suffix.

1. _____ 2. _____

3. _____

B. Write the spelling words that have the **ance** suffix.

1. _____ 2. _____

3. _____

C. Write the spelling words that have the **age** suffix.

1. _____ 2. _____

3. _____ 4. _____

D. Write the spelling words that have the **en** suffix.

1. _____ 2. _____

E. Write the spelling words that have the **some** suffix.

1. _____ 2. _____

F. Write the spelling words that have two syllables.

1. _____ 2. _____

3. _____ 4. _____

5. _____ 6. _____

A. Write all of these words in syllables using hyphens between the syllables. Use your spelling glossary.

1. enjoyable _____

2. disturbance _____

3. shortage _____

4. baggage _____

5. passage _____

6. available _____

7. postage _____

8. acceptable _____

9. insurance _____

10. assistance _____

11. wooden _____

12. sadden _____

13. tiresome _____

14. wholesome _____

B. Write these words in alphabetical order.

    available   **acceptable**   **insurance**   **assistance**

1. _____   3. _____

2. _____   4. _____

Fill in the blanks with spelling words to complete the sentences. You will need to add **ed** to one word.

1. The letter required more _____ than normal mail.

2. James was laid off because there was a _____ of work.

3. I was _____ by the news of the young man's death.

4. You should eat _____ food to stay healthy.

5. The old woman needed _____ in walking.

6. The police may be called if you cause a _____.

7. The vacation was very _____.

8. Many people booked a _____ on the Titanic.

9. I paid the bill for our _____ on the house.

10. Will you be _____ to work tomorrow?

11. Typing the whole glossary can be very _____.

12. Ms. Thompson sent a very nice letter that was _____ to me.

13. The _____ bat could hurt you if you were hit by it.

14. Is there a _____ compartment on an airplane?

Write the spelling words three times.

1. enjoyable

2. disturbance

3. shortage

4. baggage

5. passage

6. available

7. postage

8. acceptable

9. insurance

10. assistance _____   _____

_____

11. wooden   _____   _____

_____

12. sadden   _____   _____

_____

13. tiresome   _____   _____

_____

14. wholesome   _____   _____

_____

Unit 35

These spelling words contain suffixes.

1. payment
2. goodness
3. thankful
4. darkness
5. restful
6. needless
7. peaceful
8. spotless
9. kindness
10. hopeless
11. statement
12. equipment
13. careful
14. cheerful

Suffixes can change the meaning of a word. The suffix **ment** means **"the instrument of an action."** The suffix **ness** means **"quality, state or degree of."** The suffix **ful** means **"the number or quantity that would fill."** The suffix **less** means **"not having."**

Unit 35

These spelling words contain suffixes.

1. payment
2. goodness
3. thankful
4. darkness
5. restful
6. needless
7. peaceful
8. spotless
9. kindness
10. hopeless
11. statement
12. equipment
13. careful
14. cheerful

A. Write the spelling words that have the **ment** suffix.

1. _____ 2. _____

3. _____

B. Write the spelling words that have the **ness** suffix.

1. _____ 2. _____

3. _____

C. Write the spelling words that have the **ful** suffix.

1. _____ 2. _____

3. _____ 4. _____

5. _____

D. Write the spelling words that have the **less** suffix.

1. _____ 2. _____

3. _____

E. Write the spelling word that has three syllables.

_____

F. Write the spelling words that begin with a consonant cluster.

1. _____ 2. _____

A. Write these words in alphabetical order.

peaceful	payment	cheerful	thankful
hopeless	goodness	darkness	kindness
restful	spotless	careful	statement
needless	equipment		

1. _____ 8. _____

2. _____ 9. _____

3. _____ 10. _____

4. _____ 11. _____

5. _____ 12. _____

6. _____ 13. _____

7. _____ 14. _____

B. Write the words that fit the definitions.

1. _____ full of care for something

2. _____ full of cheer

3. _____ quiet, calm, full of peace

4. _____ being dark, lack of light

5. _____ kind nature, being kind

6. _____ something stated

7. _____ not needed

Use spelling words to complete the sentences.

1. I would like to have a _____ night of sleep.

2. Please be _____ to not stumble when you are walking in the _____.

3. It is _____ to talk all the time if you don't have something good to say.

4. We should be _____ for the _____ of God.

5. My house is usually _____ and quiet.

6. James ordered the _____ to tune a piano.

7. The house was so dirty that it could cause you to wonder if it would ever be _____.

8. It is nice to show _____ to visitors in your church.

9. The _____ was due on the last day of the month.

10. Was his _____ true?

11. The baby smiled so much that it would cause me to be _____.

12. Repairing the house seemed like a _____ cause.

Write the spelling words three times.

1. payment

2. goodness

3. thankful

4. darkness

5. restful

6. needless

7. peaceful

8. spotless

9. kindness

10. hopeless _____ _____

11. statement _____ _____

12. equipment _____

13. careful _____ _____

14. cheerful _____ _____

Unit 36
Review

Ask teacher for test.

Part 1 Grade _____

Part 2 Grade _____

Part 3 Grade _____

Part 4 Grade _____

Spelling Glossary Pronunciations

ă cat map

ā age, race

ä father, calm '

â care, air

ĕ red, bed

ē eat, he

ė mother, heard

ĭ is, it

ī ice, ride

ŏ hot, cot

ō over, go

ô ball, caught

oi oil, boy

ou house, out

ŭ up, cup
ū use, few
ü rule, move

ə represents.
a in about
e in taken
i in pencil
o in lemon
u in circus

A a

a-buse(ə būz′) *v.* make bad use of
I did not want anyone to abuse me.

ac-cept-a-ble(ăk sĕp′ tə bəl) *adj.* worth accepting; agreeable
I was certainly agreeable to eat popcorn.

a-corn(ā′ kôrn) *n.* a nut that grows on oak trees
Squirrels gather acorns.

a-cross(ə krôs′) *prep.* from one side to another.
I walked across the street.

ad-dress(ăd′ rĕs) *n.* a street and house number
You should know your own address.

a-gree(ə grē′) *v.* to have the same opinion
James and I agree that the weather is cold.

a-live(ə līv′) *adj.* full of life; living
Jesus is alive forever more.

a-mong(ə mŭng′) *prep.* in with
We were among the few that were in church.

an-i-mal(ăn′ ə məl) *n.* a living moving creature
We saw some animals at the zoo.

ap-pear(ə pēr′) *v.* to come into view

aren't(ärnt) the contraction for "are not"

as-sist-ance(ə sĭs′ təns) *n.* helper; aid
You could be of assistance to the old woman.

aunt(ănt) *n.* the sister or sister-in-law of one of your parents

a-ward(ə wôrd′) *n.* a prize
Whoever won the game got an award.

a-way(ə wā′) *adv.* not near

a-vail-a-ble(ə vāl′ ə bəl) *adj.* that can be used

B b

ba-by(bā′ bē) *n.* a very young child
pl. **ba-bies**
Ola had five babies.

bag-gage(băg′ ĭj) *n.* trunks, bags, or suitcases

bald

bald(bôld) *adj.* wholly or partly without hair on the head
Kevin was almost completely bald.

bare(bãr) *adj.* without covering
The trees are bare in the winter.

bar-gain(bär′ gən) *n.* something bought for a low price
I got a bargain on the shirts.

bas-ket(băs′ kĭt) *n.* a straw container
I bought a basket with artificial flowers in it.

beat(bēt) 1. *n.* a unit of time or accent in music   2. *v.* to mix rapidly

beau-ty(bū′ tē) *n.* something good to look at *pl.* **beau-ties**
Matthew would think his truck was a beauty.

beet(bēt) *n.* a white or purple vegetable
I do not know what a beet tastes like.

be-low(bĭ lō′) *adv.* under
Keep your feet below the desk.

bet-ter(bĕt′ ər) *adj.* finer
I have eaten better oranges than those.

big(bĭg) *adj.* large
bigger, biggest

brain

blank(blăngk) 1. *n.* an empty space on a paper 2. *adj.* not written upon
Fill in all the blanks on the paper.

blend(blĭnd) *v.* mix together
Please blend the cake mix for me.

blind(blīnd) *adj.* not able to see
Even though Herman was blind, he could play the organ.

blink(blĭnk) *v.* to wink very fast
Don't blink your eyes when your picture is being taken.

bone(bōn) *n.* a piece of the skeleton
The upper arm bone is called the humerus.

bore(bôr) *v.* to bother by being dull and uninteresting **bored**
It is easy to get bored while listening to some speakers.

book(buk) *n.* pieces of paper held together along an edge
I had been reading the book.

bought(bôt) *v.* did buy
We bought the white van.

brain(brān) *n.* the body's main nerve center that directs a person's thoughts and actions
I have a model of the brain.

brave

brave(brāv) *adj.* courageous
David was very brave to kill the giant.
braver, bravest

break(brāk) *v.* to damage by tearing or cracking
Wind can break windows in a house.

brook(bruk) *n.* a small stream
David chose five stones from the brook.

build(bĭld) *v.* to make
James can build a trailer.

bunch(bŭnch) *n.* a group of things
I have a bunch of notebooks.

bur-ro(bėr′ ō) *n.* a small donkey
Would you like to ride a burro?

but-ter(bŭt′ ər) *n.* a dairy product like cream
She left some butter with us.

C c

cab-in(kăb′ən) *n.* a small roughly built house
Abraham Lincoln lived in a log cabin.

cal-en-dar(koul′ ən dər) *n.* a table showing the months, weeks, and days of the year
I have a calendar hanging in the living room.

cellar

calf(kăf) *n.* a young cow
pl. calves

cam-el(kăm′ əl) *n.* a desert animal with one or two humps
I saw a camel at the zoo.

can-ner-y(kăn′ ər ē) *n.* a place where food is put into cans

care-ful(kãr′ fəl) *adj.* not taking chances
Please be careful when mowing grass.

car-ry(kãr′ ē) *v.* to transport or move something from one place to another
Kevin could carry his lunch to work.
car-ried, car-ry-ing

cas-tle(kăs′ əl) *n.* the home of a king or queen.
Did Princess Diana live in a castle?

cel-er-y(sĕl′ ər ē) *n.* a light green vegetable in a stalk
James likes to eat celery with peanut butter.

cel-lar(sĕl′ ər) *n.* a basement or underground room
They went to the cellar when there was a tornado.

chase

chase(chās) *v.* to run after someone
Who will you chase if you are playing tag?
chased, chas-ing

cheer(chēr) 1. *n.* a sound of encouragement 2. *v.* to give a cheer
We could give a cheer for the graduates.

cheer-ful(chēr′ fəl) *adj.* full of cheer; glad

chick-en(chĭk′ ən) *n.* a farm bird that is used for eggs and meat
Donna fed the chickens.

child(chīld) *n.* a very young person
Jennifer had one child.
pl. chil-dren

child-hood(chīld′ hud) *n.* the time of a person's life from birth to adulthood
You should go to church during your childhood.

chirp(chėrp) *n.* a bird sound
Can you hear a bird chirp outside?

church(chėrch) *n.* a building for public Christian worship
We have a church in Louisville, Kentucky.

cough

churn(chėrn) 1. *n.* a butter-making container
Please make the butter in the churn.
2. *v.* to stir with force.
Churn the butter for me, please.

clear(klēr) *adj.* easy to see through *adv.* easy to understand

col-lar(kŏl′ ər) *n.* the part of a shirt around the neck.
I wanted James to put his collar down.

col-or(kŭl′ ər) 1. *n.* red, blue, yellow, etc. One of the seven parts of the rainbow
What color is your hair?
2. *v.* to put color on something
Please color a picture for me.

comb(kōm) *n.* an object with teeth used to arrange hair
I used a comb to get tangles out of my hair.

cop-per(kŏp′ ər) *n.* a reddish metal
Some water pipes are made of copper.

cop-y(kŏp′ ē) *v.* to write the same thing twice **cop-ied, cop-y-ing**

cough(kôf) *v.* to force air from the lungs with sudden effort and noise
I usually cough if I have a cold.

course(kôrs) *n.* a direction taken
Which course do you plan to take if you walk in the woods?

crack(krăk) *n.* a small break
Did you see the crack in the egg?

cream(krēm) *n.* the thick part of milk that contains butterfat
Scoop the cream off the top of the milk.

crease(krēs) *v.* to make a line by folding
Crease the paper in half.
creased, creas-ing

crumb(krŭm) *n.* a little piece of something
Pick up the crumb off the floor.

cute(kūt) *adj.* charming; nice looking
The puppy was cute.

D d

dair-y(dãr′ ē) *n.* a place where milk, cream, cheese, and butter are sold
We bought milk at the dairy.

damp(dămp) *adj.* a little wet
The grass was damp.

dark-ness(därk′nĭs) *n.* being dark; lack of light
It is hard for people to see you if you are walking in the darkness with dark clothes.

day-light(dā′ līt) *n.* the light from the sun

day(dā) *n.* the time when the sun is up
James washed the van during the day. *pl. days*

de-cide(dĭ sīd′) *v.* to make up your mind **de-cid-ed, de-cid-ing**

de-lay(dĭ lā′) *n.* a wait before something
We might have a short delay at the bus station.
pl. delays

dirt-y(dėr′ tē) *adj,* not clean
Benjamin's face was dirty.

dis-ap-pear(dĭs ə pēr′) *v.* to move out of sight
It seemed like James disappeared out of my sight.

dis-turb-ance(dĭs tėr′ bəns) *n.* a thing that disturbs
The car's muffler was a disturbance.

doc-tor(dŏk′ tər) *n.* a person who helps sick people get better
I went to see the doctor after I felt dizzy.

doesn't(dŭz′ ənt) contraction for does not

dolphin

dol-phin(dŏl′ fən) *n.* a small whale that has a snout like a beak
Dolphins like to jump out of the water.

don-key(dŏng′ kē) *n.* an animal that looks something like a small horse with long ears
Jesus rode on a donkey.

E e

ea-gle(ē′ gəl) *n.* a large bird that can see far and has strong wings
The eagle is the symbol for the United States.

el-bow(ĕl′ bō) *n.* the joint in the arm
I hit my elbow on the door facing.

e-lev-en(ĭ lĕv′ ən) *n., adj.* one more than ten
There were eleven students.

emp-ty(ĕmp′ tē) *adj.* having nothing inside
Make sure your glass is empty before taking it to the kitchen.

en-joy(ĕn joi′) *v.* to have a good time
en joyed, en-joy-ing

en-joy-a-ble(ĕn joi′ ə bəl) *adj.* able to have a good time

farther

e-nough(ĭ nŭf′) *adj.* having as many as needed.
We had enough money to buy the bike.

en-ter(ĕn′ tər) *v.* to go into a place
Please enter the correct door.

e-quip-ment(ĭ kwĭp′ mənt) *n.* necessary tools for the job
He had the equipment to weld the trailer.

er-rand(ĕr′ ənd) *n.* a trip to get something

er-ror(ĕr′ ər) *n.* a mistake
Tell me if you find an error on a worksheet.

e-ven(ē′ vən) 1. *adj.* not odd
Two, four, and six are even numbers
2. smooth or level

eve-ry(ĕv′ rē) *adj.* each one

F f

fam-i-ly(făm′ ə lē) *n.* a group of people related to each other

far-ther(fär′ th ər) *adj.* more distant

fat

fat(făt) *adj.* having much of a white or yellow substance formed in our body
I knew I was too fat when I stepped on the scale. **fat-ter, fat-test**

fa-vor(fā′ vər) 1. *n.* a kindness
Please do me a favor by getting me some milk.
2. *v.* to prefer
I favor apples more than peaches.

field(fēld) *n.* a pasture
There were two ponies in the field.

fine(fīn) *adj.* very good; thin
The dress was a fine dress for me.
fin-er, fin-est

flight(flīt) *n.* movement through the air

foot(fut) *n.* the part of the body at the end of the leg
James's foot was broken.

foot-step(fut′ stĕp) *n.* the sound of feet walking

force(fôrs) *v.* putting strength against something
Do not force the foot into the shoe.
forced, forc-ing

geese

four-teen(fôr tēn′) *n.* the number after thirteen.

fourth(fôrth) *adj.* next after third; one of four equal parts.
Anthony was her fourth child.

freeze(frēz) *v.* to turn something into ice.
We could freeze the orange juice.

full(ful) *adj.* filled
Please fill the cup with milk, so it will be full.

fun-nies(fŭn′ ēz) *n.* the comics
James likes to read the funnies.

fur-ther(fėr′ thər) *adj.* more
Ask me if you need further help.

G g

ga-rage(gə räzh′) *n.* a place for keeping a car
Please park the van in the garage.

gath-er(găth′ ər) *v.* to bring things together
Would you gather artificial flowers for me?

geese(gēs) *n.* more than one goose

gleam

gleam(glēm) 1. *n.* a shine
I could see the gleam in his eyes.

gold(gōld) *n.* a valuable yellow metal
Some people have gold in their teeth.

good-ness(gud′nĭs) *n.* the state of being good
We have no goodness except what God gives us.

goose(güs) *n.* a bird that is similar to a duck
Have you ever seen one goose by itself?

grand(grănd) *adj.* large; dignified
The grand piano sounds beautiful.

grind(grīnd) *v.* to crush into small pieces

groan(grōn) *n.* a sound of pain

guard(gärd) 1. *v.* to protect
2. *n.* a person who protects

guess(gĕs) 1. *n.* a choice made without much information 2. *v.* to make a guess
Guess what we're having for supper.

guest (gĕst) 1. *n.* a person that is a visitor
I was a guest in the school.

hoarse

guide(gīd) 1. *n.* a person who shows the way
2. *v.* to show someone the way

guilt-y(gĭl′tē) *adj.* having done something wrong
The man was guilty of making drugs.

gui-tar(gĭ tär′) *n.* a musical instrument with strings that are plucked
I would like to learn to play the guitar.

H h

hand-y(hăn′dē) *adj.* good at making things
James is handy at fixing things.

he'd(hēd) contraction for he would

height(hīt) *n.* tallness

her-o(hēr′ō) *n.* a very brave person
David was a hero for his people.

hoarse(hôrs) *adj.* sounding rough and deep

honey

hon-ey(hŭn′ ē) *n.* a sweet substance made by bees
You can put honey on your toast.

hon-or(ŏn′ ər) *n.* recognition for doing a good job
Mr. Taylor received the honor of being the main speaker.

hood(hud) *n.* a cover for the head
The blue jacket had a hood on it.

hope-less(hōp′ lĭs) *adj.* feeling no hope
Having cancer is not always hopeless.

horse(hôrs) *n.* a four-legged animal with a mane and a tail and solid hoofs
Tina rode a horse.

ho-tel(hō tĕl′) *n.* a building where people pay to stay overnight
We stayed in a hotel in Tennessee.

how'd(houd) a contraction for how would or how did
How'd you like going on that trip?

huge(hūj) *adj.* very large
An elephant is a huge animal.

hun-dred(hŭn′ drəd) *n. adj.* the number 100
I had one hundred pennies.

key

I i

I'd(īd) contraction for I would.
I'd like to go to sleep earlier tonight.

im-por-tant(ĭm pôrt′ ənt) *adj.* serious
It is important for you to get an education.

ink(ĭngk) *n.* a colored liquid used for writing
Ben had a lot of ink on him from a pen.

in-sur-ance(ĭn shür′ əns) *n.* money to be paid for a loss
I paid insurance on the house in case it burned.

J j

jeer(jēr) *v.* to make fun in a rude or unkind way
It is not nice to jeer at an handicapped person.

jour-nal(jėr′ nəl) *n.* a newspaper or diary
Anne Frank kept a journal of her life when she was hiding.

jour-ney(jėr′ nē) *n.* a trip
Columbus went on a journey to find the Indies.

K k

key(kē) *n.* a piece of metal that opens or closes a lock

kindness

kind-ness(kīnd′ nĭs) *n.* being kind; a kind nature
We showed kindness to Frankie after the death of his mother.

knee(nē) *n.* the joint between the thigh and the calf of the leg
I skinned my knee when I had the bike wreck.

kneel(nēl) *v.* to get down on your knees
Sometimes I kneel down to pray.

knife(nīf) *n.* a cutting utensil
pl. knives
I cut a tomato with a knife.

knob(nŏb) *n.* a round handle
Turn the knob on the door.

knock(nŏk) *v.* to tap on something
Byron has learned to knock on the door.

know(nō) *v.* to be certain of something I know who Jimmy is.

L l

lace(lās) *n.* an open weaving or net of fine thread in an ornamental pattern
I put lace on the pink dresses.

lad-der(lăd′ ər) *n.* steps fastened between two long boards
James stood on the ladder to fix the ceiling.

life

lamb(lăm) *n.* a young sheep

large(lärj) *adj.* big
The Titanic was a large ship.
larg-er, larg-est

laugh(lăf) *v.* to make the sounds and movement of showing joy
I laugh at funny things that toddlers do.

leaf(lēf) *n.* the thin, flat, green part of a tree

learn(lėrn) *v.* to gain knowledge or skill
I would like to learn to play the piano better.

leath-er(lĕth′ ər) *n.* a material made from the skins of certain animals
Frankie said the man wore a leather jacket even in summer.

lem-on(lĕm′ ən) *n.* a sour yellow fruit that grows in warm climates
You can make lemonade from lemons.

li-brar-y(lī′ brăr ē) *n.* a room or building where collections of books, magazines, and movies are kept. *pl. libraries*
We checked out two books from the library.

life((līf) *n.* the state of being alive. *pl. lives*

listen

lis-ten(lĭs′ ən) *v.* to try to hear
I like to listen to Gospel music.

liv-er(lĭv ′ ər) *n.* an organ that helps the body use food.
The liver is the largest internal organ of the body.

M m

mad(măd) *adj.* angry
Being hit in the face could make you mad.
mad-der, mad-dest

mail(māl) *n.* letters, cards, and parcels to be sent
I had four pieces of mail today.

male(māl) *n.* a boy or man
Patti has had one male child.

mar-ble(mär′ bəl) *n.* a small glass ball
Small children should not play with a marble.

mar-ry(măr′ ē) *v.* to join as husband and wife
mar-ried, mar-ry-ing
We planned to marry in December.

mat-ter(măt′ ər) *v.* to be important
How he fixes the bathroom will matter.

mend(měnd) *v.* to repair or fix something
I knew I should mend the dress.

music

mer-ry(měr′ ē) *adj.* jolly; full of fun

might(mīt) *n.* a great force
Goliath thought he had a lot of might.

mind(mīnd) 1. *n.* the part of a person that thinks
Use your mind when doing math.
2. *v.* to care for
Do you mind getting some milk for me?

mist(mĭst) *n.* a light fog
Sometimes it is hard to see through a mist.

mit-ten(mĭt′ ən) *n.* a warm covering for the hand. *pl. mittens*
Mittens will help keep your hands warm.

mon-ey(mŭn′ ē) *n.* coins or paper used for buying things
David and Jimmy counted their money.

mon-key(mŭng′ kē) *n.* an animal that looks like a small ape. *pl. monkeys*

mound(mound) *n.* a small hill or pile of earth
She left a mound of earth over the grave.

mu-sic(mū′ zĭk) *n.* the art of making sounds that are beautiful

N n

need-less(nēd′ lĭs) *adj.* not needed, unnecessary
It is needless to use bad language.

neph-ew(nĕf′ ū) *n.* the son of one's brother or sister.
Kenny is my nephew.

nev-er(nĕv′ ər) *adv.* at no time
I never want to be charged with murder.

nice(nīs) *adj.* pleasing and kind
I want to be nice to people.
nic-er, nic-est

no-tice(nō ′ tĭs) *v.* to pay attention to
Did you notice that the twins had gotten a haircut? **no-ticed, no-tic-ing**

num-ber(nŭm′ bər) *n.* a numeral
One thousand is a large number.

O o

oak(ōk) *n.* a tree with hard wood and acorns
Do you have an oak tree in your yard?

oar(ôr) *n.* a paddle used to row a boat
The life boats needed oars to be with them.

o-a-sis(ō ā′ sĭs) *n.* a fertile place in a desert

of-ten(ô′ fən) *adv.* many times
I often eat breakfast early.

or-der(ôr′ dər) 1. *n.* a command
The lesson plans were the order of work for them to do
2. *v.* to command
I gave the order to get to work.

or-phan(ôr′ fən) *n.* a child whose parents are dead
Shura was an orphan after her mother and father had died.

ov-en(ŭv′ ən) *n.* a space in a stove used for baking
I baked the chicken in the oven.

o-ver(ō′ vər) *adv.* above
The tree branches were hanging over the house.

P p

pain(pān) *n.* an ache, an uncomfortable feeling
I have a pain in my back.

pam-phlet(păm′ flĭt) *n.* a booklet in paper covers
Have you read a pamphlet about measles?

pa-per(pā ′ pər) *n.* a material used for writing, printing, or wrapping something

paragraph

par-a-graph(pãr′ ə grăf) *n.* a group of sentences that belong together
Please write a paragraph about what you did over the weekend.

par-ent(pãr′ ənt) *n.* a father or mother

pas-sage(păs′ ĭj) *n.* a hall or way through a building
We walked down the passage to the restroom.

pay-ment(pā′ mənt) *n.* amount paid
I paid the payment on the last day of the month.

peace-ful(pēs′ fəl) *adj.* quiet; calm
It is peaceful at our house most of the time.

pear(pãr) *n.* a fruit
I would rather have an apple than a pear.

pen-cil(pĕn′ səl) *n.* a writing tool
Always use a pencil to fill in the voter's ballet.

pen-ny(pĕn′ ē) *n.* a coin worth one cent
pl. pennies

pep-per(pĕp′ ər) *n.* a hot seasoning for food
Many people put black pepper on their potatoes.

pint

per-i-od(pēr′ ē əd) *n.* a punctuation mark at the end of a telling sentence
Don't forget to put the period at the end of each telling sentence.

pest(pĕst) *n.* someone or something that causes problems
Ants can be a pest in the kitchen.

phon-ics(fŏn′ ĭks) *n.* a method of teaching people to learn to read
I taught phonics in my school.

pho-to(fō′ tō) *n.* a picture made with a camera
He took a photo of the piano.

phrase(frāz) *n.* a combination of words; an expression
" A penny saved is a penny earned" is a phrase that has been known for a long time.

pi-an-o(pē ăn′ ō) *n.* a musical instrument with white and black keys
I love to play the piano.

pile(pīl) *n.* a heap or mound
Beverly made a pile of leaves.

pi-lot(pī′ lət) *n.* a person who flies a plane or runs a boat

pint(pīnt) *n.* half of a quart

pioneer

pi-o-neer(pī ə nēr′) *n.* one of the first settlers
Daniel Boone was a pioneer.

plan-et(plăn′ ĭt) *n.* a body moving around the sun
Earth is the planet on which we live.

play(plā) *v.* to participate in a game
I like to play kickball.
played, play-ing

please(plēs) *v.* to make someone happy
We should want to please God.

plur-al(plur′ əl) *n. adj.* two or more
"Pens" is the plural of "pen."

pock-et(pŏk ĭt) *n.* a little bag sewn into clothes
I put my keys into my pocket.

po-ny(pō′ nē) *n.* a small horse
pl. ponies

porch(pôrch) *n.* a roofed entrance
James made our porch bigger.

post(pōst) *n.* a pole
James fastened fence to a post.

post-age(pōs′ tĭj) *n.* amount paid on something sent by mail
I paid the extra postage for the letter.

queen

pre-pare(prĭ pãr′) *v.* to make ready
She should prepare to get ready for church.

pro-gram(prō′ grăm) *n.* the order of events at a show
The graduation program was a beautiful ceremony.

pu-pil(pū′ pəl) *n.* a learner or student
Mara was a pupil in our school.

pup-pet(pūp′ ĭt) *n.* a doll that is moved by a person
They had a puppet show for Vacation Bible School.

put(put) *v.* to place a thing
I put my keys on the shelf.

Q q

qual-i-fied(kwŏl′ ə fīd) *adj.* fitted; competent
I felt like I was qualified for the job.

quar-rel(kwôr′ əl) *n.* an argument
We should not quarrel with others.

quar-ter(kwôr′ tər) *n.* a coin worth twenty-five cents

queen(kwēn) *n.* the female ruler of some countries
Queen Victoria was a nice queen.

ques-tion(kwĕs′ chən) *n.* an asking sentence

quick(kwĭk) *adj.* fast
Let's get a quick nap.

qui-et(kwī′ ĕt) *adj.* the absence of loud noise
Most people are quiet when they sleep.

qui-et-ness(kwī′ ĕt nĭs) *n.* a quiet condition; calmness
There was quietness after all the students left school.

quit-ter(kwĭt′ ər) *n.* someone who gives up easily

R r

race(rās) *v.* to run quickly to outrun others
raced, rac-ing

rail-road(rāl′ rōd) *n.* a system that runs trains
My dad worked for the railroad.

raise(rāz) *v.* to lift up
Please raise the window shade.

rath-er(răth′ ər) *adv.* more willingly
I would rather eat eggs for breakfast than chicken.

ray(rā) *n.* a thin beam of light
A ray of sunlight shined through the storm door. *pl. rays*

rear(rēr) *n.* the back part
Byron walked behind the rear of the van.

reg-u-lar(rĕg′ yə lər) *adj.* normal; usual
Our walk started out in the regular way.

rein-deer(rān′ dēr) *n.* a kind of deer that lives in the northern part of North America
I have seen a picture of a reindeer.

re-main(rĭ mān′) *v.* to stay in a place
Please remain in your seat.

re-ply(rĭ plī′) *v.* to answer
Charles finally sent a reply to my question.
re-plied, re-ply-ing

rest-ful(rĕst′ fəl) *adj.* full of rest
You should have a restful night of sleep.

rich(rĭch) *adj.* having much money
Most presidents are rich.

rob-in(rŏb′ ən) *n.* an American bird with reddish feathers on its chest

rough(rŭf) *adj.* not smooth
Sandpaper is rough.

rum-ble(rŭm′ bəl) *n.* a deep, heavy continuous sound
We could hear the rumble of a train.

S s

sad-den(săd′ ən) *v.* to make sad
The death of the baby was enough to sadden us.

sail(sāl) *n.* a piece of cloth that is used to catch the wind to make a boat move

sale(sāl) *v.* the act of selling
The house was for sale.

sank(săngk) *v.* did sink; went under the water

scold(skōld) *v.* to find fault with someone; to reprimand
A mother may scold a child if they run away.

scrap(skrăp) *n.* a small piece of something
We found a scrap of paper in the ditch.

scrap-book(skrăp′ buk) *n.* a book in which pictures or clippings are glued.

scratch(skrăch) *v.* to rub a place that itches
Do not scratch your arm if you touch poison ivy.

scream(skrēm) *v.* to cry out
Some people scream if they get scared.

screen(skrēn) *n.* a woven material to keep insects out
Put a screen on the window.

scrub(skrŭb) *v.* to rub hard while washing something
Scrub your arm to get the dirt off.

seam(sēm) *n.* the line along which two things join
I sewed the seam in the dress.

search(sėrch) *v.* to look for something
Please help me search for my keys.

shape(shāp) *v.* to form something
shaped, shap-ing

share(shãr) *v.* to use something together with someone else
It is nice to share your food with someone who doesn't have any.

shears(shērz) *n.* large scissors
You can use shears to cut a sheep's wool.

she'd(shēd) contraction for she would or she had
She'd call me if she wanted to call.

she'll(shēl) contraction for she will
She'll usually answer my messages.

shook(shuk) *v.* did shake

short

short(shôrt) *adj.* not tall or not long
Mrs. Victoria knows she is short.

short-age(shôr′ tĭj) *n.* a lack of something; not enough
Sometimes I feel like I have a shortage of patience.

should(shud) *v.* used to express future time
We should go to bed earlier.

sight(sīt) *n.* power of seeing
Herman lost his sight because of an accident when he was a young boy.

sign(sīn) *n.* a thing with a printed message on it
James made a sign for our yard sale.

si-lent(sī′ lənt) *adj.* perfectly quiet
Please be silent while we are listening to the news.

silk(sĭlk) *n.* a fine soft thread spun by silkworms

sil-ly(sĭl′ ē) *adj.* foolish
Some boys like to act silly.

sim-i-lar(sĭm′ ə lər) *adj.* almost the same; very much alike
James and Dewayne looked similar when they were teenagers.

square

sink(sĭngk) *n.* a basin for washing your hands

si-ren(sī′ rən) *n.* a horn that makes a loud noise on firetrucks and ambulances
I heard the sirens and looked out the window.

skate(skāt) *n.* a shoe with wheels or a blade

sock(sŏk) *n.* a covering for the foot
pl. socks

soft-en(sôf′ ən) *v.* to make soft
You can soften butter by heating it for a few seconds in a microwave.

some(sŭm) *adj.* not all; a part of
I have some bubble gum.

speed(spēd) *n.* a rate of movement
My speed was below 70 miles per hour.

spoke(spōk) *v.* did speak
The teacher spoke with the parent.

sport(spôrt) *n.* a game needing skill and physical exercise. *pl. sports*

spot-less(spŏt′ lĭs) *adj.* without a spot of dirt
The wedding gown looked spotless.

square(skwãr) *n.* a shape with four equal sides

squash

squash(skwŏsh) 1. *n.* a yellow vegetable that is bulb-shaped at one end
I love to eat baked squash.
2. *v.* to crush
Do not squash the baby.

squaw(skwŏ) *n.* an American Indian woman
Pocahontas was a squaw.

squeak(skwēk) *v.* to make a short, shrill sound

squeal(skwēl) 1. *n.* a sharp piercing sound.
2. *v.* to make a high piercing sound.
The child likes to squeal with delight.

squeeze(skwēz) *v.* to press hard like hugging
I like to squeeze the baby.

squirm((skwėrm) *v.* to wiggle and twist
Benjamin began to squirm when he saw his grandpa's van.

squir-rel(skwėr′ əl) *n.* a small animal with a bushy tail that likes to climb trees
We saw a squirrel today when we were walking.

straight

stage(stāj) *n.* a period of development
Some babies go through a stage of cutting teeth.
2. a raised platform
We stood on the stage and sang.

state-ment(stāt′ mənt) *n.* something stated or reported
I would like to have a statement from Mrs. Beverly about my performance.

stay(stā) *v.* to remain
We will stay at home for a little while.
stayed, stay-ing

steak(stāk) *n.* a cut of meat
I like to eat pork steak.

stock(stŏk) *v.* to supply
I don't like to go to the store when it is time to stock the shelves.

sto-ry(stôr′ ē) *n.* something told about a situation. *pl. stories*
I told the boys the story of David and Goliath.

storm(stôrm) *n.* a strong wind, usually with rain, snow or thunder and lightning
I do not like to drive in a storm.

straight(strāt) *adj.* not crooked; no curves or bends

strain(strān) 1. *n.* a great effort
The strain of lifting the piano was too much for me. 2. *v.* to try very hard

strange(strānj) *adj.* not familiar
To see a man wearing a skirt is strange.

strap(străp) *n.* a strip of some material
The seat belt was a strap to keep us safe.

stray(strā) 1. *n.* a dog or cat without a home
I did not want to go near a stray dog.
2. *v.* to wander as if you are lost
Please do not stray too far from an adult.

stream(strēm) 1. *n.* a little river or large brook
The stream was flowing swiftly.
2. *v.* to flow steadily and swiftly like a river
We watched the water stream like a waterfall.

strike(strīk) 1. *v.* to hit something
I saw him strike a nail with a hammer.
2. *n.* a kick that is missed in kickball

string(strĭng) *n.* a thick thread
Use some string to fly a kite.

strong(strông) *adj.* having much strength

strum(strŭm) *v.* to sweep the fingers over the strings of a musical instrument
Isaiah would strum the guitar.

sum(sŭm) *n.* the answer to an addition problem
The sum of ten plus five is fifteen.

sum-mer(sŭm′ ər) *n.* the season after spring

sup-plies(sŭp′ plīz) *n.* necessary things for a job
I keep school supplies handy.

sur-face(sėr′ fĭs) *n.* the top or outside of something
I rubbed the surface of the piano with a cloth.

sur-prise(sėr prīz′) 1. *n.* something not expected 2. a feeling caused by an unexpected thing

T t

ta-ble(tā′ bəl) *n.* a piece of furniture with a flat top and legs
I cleaned the top of the table.

tail(tāl) *n.* the part of an animal's body that sticks out of the back
Some dogs wag their tail.

tale

tale(tāl) *n.* an untrue story
We should not tell a tale.

tear(tēr) *n.* a drop of water coming from the eye.
I saw a tear go down his cheek.

tear-ing(târ′ ĭng) *v.* pulling apart by force
The shredder was tearing the paper apart.

teeth(tēth) *n.* more than one tooth
The woman has four false teeth.

tel-e-phone(tĕl′ ə fōn) *n.* a machine for sending sound or speech by electricity
I called her on the telephone.

ten-nis(tĕn′ ĭs) *n.* a game played with a ball and rackets on a court

thank-ful(thăngk′ fəl) *adj.* feeling thanks
I am thankful for the food I have.

they'd(thād) contraction for they had or they would
They'd have laughed if they'd been there.

they'll(thāl) a contraction for they will
They'll be quiet tonight.

thirst-y(thėr′ stē) *adj.* dry from a lack of water
I liked the cold water when I was thirsty.

toy

thorn(thôrn) *n.* a pointed growth on the stem of a rose bush
It was not pleasant to have a thorn stuck in my hand.

ti-ny(tī′ nē) *adj.* very small
The newborn baby was tiny.

tire-some(tīr′ sŭm) *adj.* a thing that causes one to feel bored or annoyed
It is tiresome to type more than three hundred definitions.

to-night(tə nīt′) *n.* this night
I am tired tonight.

took(tuk) *v.* did take; grasped
I took the little boy home.

tooth(tuth) *n.* one of the hard bone-like parts of the mouth used for chewing

top-coat(tŏp′ kōt) *n.* a lightweight coat
James has a long topcoat.

tor-na-do(tôr nā ′ dō) *n.* a strong whirlwind
The tornado passed close to the church.

tough(tŭf) *adj.* being able to bend without breaking

toy(toi) *n.* something to play with
pl. toys

trade

trade(trād) *v.* an exchange of one thing for another
I do not want the students to trade their lunches.

trav-el(trăv′ əl) *v.* to go from one place to another
We like to travel to camp meetings.

tray(trā) *n.* a flat shallow holder with a rim around it. *pl. trays*
Put all of the food on the tray.

twirl(twėrl) *v.* to spin around rapidly
It can make you dizzy to twirl around.

U u

un-done(ŭn dŭn′) *adj.* not done

un-fair(ŭn fãr′) *adj.* not fair

use(ūz) *v.* to put into service or action
Please use the scissors carefully.

V v

val-ley(voul′ ē) *n.* low land between mountains or hills
pl. valleys

vis-i-tor(vĭz′ ə tər) *n.* a person who visits
Mr. Poindexter was a visitor in our school.

woman

W w

wag-on(wăg′ ən) *n.* a four-wheeled cart
Daniel Boone's friends traveled in wagons.

we'll(wēl) contraction for we will.
We'll be wanting to go to sleep tonight.

what's(hwŏts) contraction for what is
What's your name?

whis-tle(hwĭs′ əl) 1. *n.* a high sounding shrill sound made by forcing air through the teeth. 2. *v.* to make a whistling sound.

who'd(hüd) a contraction for who would or who did
Who'd we talk to?

whole-some(hōl′ sŭm) *adj.* healthful
Eat good wholesome food.

who's(hüz) contraction for who is
Who's in the restroom?

wild(wīld) *adj.* living or growing in forests; not tame
Most lions are wild.

wink(wĭngk) *v.* to close the eye and open quickly

wom-an(wôm′ ən) *n.* an adult female person *pl. wom-en*
Mrs. Thompson is a woman.

women

wom-en(wĭm′ ən) *n.* more than one woman
There were seven women working in the room.

wood(wud) *n.* the hard substance found under the bark of a tree
Wood is used to make houses.

wood-chuck(wud′ chŭk) *n.* a small furry animal with a bushy tail

wood-en(wud′ ən) *adj.* made of wood
Monica had a wooden baby bed.

wool(wul) *n.* the soft hair of sheep

work-er(wėrk′ ər) *n.* a person who works
James is a hard worker.

would(wud) *v.* will
Would you turn on the light?

wreck(rĕk) *n.* something that is badly damaged

wrin-kle(rĭng′ kəl) *v.* to crease
Please do not wrinkle your paper.

wrist(rĭst) *n.* the joint between the hand and the arm.

write(rīt) *v.* to put words on paper
You may write a letter to your mother.

wrong(rŏng) *adj.* not right

Y y

year(yēr) *n.* twelve months

you'd(ūd) contraction for you would

Z z

zero(zēr′ ō) *n.* the number that stands for nothing

Unit 6
Review of lessons 1-5
Part 1

Circle the letter of the correct spelling for the word that belongs in the blank.

1. There was a _____ in the concrete.

    A. crack B. crake C. crak

2. You should know your own _____.

    A. adress B. addrass C. address

3. We should _____ use drugs.

    A. naver B. never C. nevir

4. Black _____ is hot.

    A. peper B. pepper C. papper

5. A _____ can store water in its hump.

    A. camel B. camil C. cammel

6. Wash our hands in the _____.

    A. senk B. sienk C. sink

7.. I do not want an _____ living in our house.

    A. anemal B. animal C. annimal

8. Sometimes the rain is like a fine _____.

    A. mest B. misst C. mist

9. We should read our Bible _____ day.

    A. evere   B. eviry   C. every

10. Some people like to _____ across the country.

    A. travel   B. treval   C. travell

11. The grass is _____ in the morning.

    A. damp   B. demp   C. dammp

12. Sometimes boys enjoy being a _____.

    A. past   B. pest   C. peast

13. The mayor is _____.

    A. rech   B. rish   C. rich

14. Carpet and a rug are both _____ floor coverings.

    A. similer   B. similar   C. semilar

15. Kevin was able to _____ his own clothes.

    A. mind   B. mennd   C. mend

16. Check to see if the bikes are in the _____.

    A. garoge   B. garage   C. garege

17. The name of our _____ is Earth.

    A. planet   B. planit   C. plenit

18. _____ we walk on the road at nighttime?

    A. shood   B. shoud   C. should

Unit 6
Review of lessons 1-5
Part 2

Circle the letter of the correct spelling for the word that belongs in the blank.

1. We could hear the _____ of a train.

   A. rumbel　　　　　B. rumbble　　　　　C. rumble

2. James went to the _____ because he had poison ivy.

   A. doctor　　　　　B. docktor　　　　　C. docter

3. Abraham Lincoln was born in a _____.

   A. cabbin　　　　　B. cabin　　　　　C. caben

4. Lee got a six foot _____.

   A. ladder　　　　　B. lader　　　　　C. laddre

5. _____ will help your hands stay warm in the winter.

   A. mittins　　　　　B. mittens　　　　　C. mitens

6. James bought a _____ for the little.

   A. toppcoat　　　　　B. topcaot　　　　　C. topcoat

7. We get some _____ shoes for David.

   A. tenis　　　　　B. tinnis　　　　　C. tennis

8. I plan to buy _____ for the dinner.

   A. chicken　　　　　B. chiken　　　　　C. chickin

9. The _____ is the largest organ inside the body.

    A. livir   B. liver   C. livver

10. I bought a _____ of grapes.

    A. bunch   B. bunsh   C. bunnch

11. Did you find a one _____ dollar bill?

    A. hundrid   B. hunndred   C. hundred

12. Would you like to _____ the guitar?

    A. strrum   B. strum   C. stum

13. The dishes were _____ when I left.

    A. undune   B. undone   C. undun

14. Jimmy knew where the _____ were.

    A. socks   B. soks   C. sooks

15. Have you seen a _____'s nest?

    A. roben   B. robbin   C. robin

16. Did that store have a _____ opening sale the first day it was open?

    A. grend   B. grand   C. grrand

17. Have you ever felt of _____ material?

    A. silk   B. sielk   C. sillk

18. Please use a _____ for the test.

    A. pincel   B. pencil   C. pincil

Unit 6
Review of lessons 1-5
Part 3

Circle the letter of the correct spelling for the word that belongs in the blank.

1. The keys were in my _____.

    A. pockit   B. pocket   C. poket

2. Some nouns form the _____ by adding **s**.

    A. plural   B. plooral   C. plurul

3. David chose five stones from a _____.

    A. brook   B. bruke   C. brooke

4. _____ comes from sheep.

    A. Woole   B. Wull   C. Wool

5. We could take a _____ of food and go on a picnic.

    A. bascet   B. basket   C. bassket

6. I did not want a _____ couch.

    A. leether   B. leather   C. leathre

7. Greg _____ my hand.

    A. shoke   B. shuke   C. shook

8. The container had been _____.

    A. empty   B. emppty   C. empte

9. Do they _____ the shelves on Friday night?

    A. stoke   B. stocke   C. stock

10. The sweater did not have a _____ on it.

    A. hud   B. hoode   C. hood

11. It is near the end of _____.

    A. sumer   B. summer   C. sommer

12. If you eat too much, you will feel _____.

    A. foul   B. full   C. fule

13. It looked like a spider had bitten my _____.

    A. foot   B. fute   C. fout

14. I _____ the stamp on the envelope.

    A. pute   B. poot   C. put

15. Zach _____ the permit test.

    A. tooke   B. took   C. touk

16. Do you want a slice of _____ in your tea?

    A. lemon   B. lemun   C. limon

17. He used _____ pipes for the water lines.

    A. coper   B. coppur   C. copper

Unit 6
Review of lessons 1-5
Part 4

Circle the letter of the correct spelling for the word that belongs in the blank.

1. Sarah is almost _____ years old.

   A. elevin   B. eliven   C. eleven

2. I have a large toaster _____.

   A. oven   B. aven   C. ovin

3. We had a little red _____.

   A. wegan   B. wagon   C. wagun

4. _____ grows as a green stalk.

   A. selery   B. celery   C. celiry

5. Children are expected to play during their _____.

   A. childhood   B. childhud   C. chilldhood

6. Who sat _____ the table from you?

   A. akross   B. acros   C. across

7. A _____ reunion should be a time of fun.

   A. family   B. famely   C. famile

8. Guess a _____ between one and ten.

   A. numbre   B. numbber   C. number

9. Do not talk to strangers; walk _____ from them.

    A. uway   B. awway   C. away

10. Be _____ when others are talking.

    A. silint   B. silent   C. sillent

11. Always respect a _____.

    A. parent   B. pareent   C. parint

12. Be _____ when walking on ice.

    A. careful   B. carful   C. carefull

13. A _____ is a small furry animal.

    A. woodchuk   B. woodchuck   C. wudchuck

14. The glossary is in the back of the _____.

    A. boock   B. bock   C. book

15. Shauna was not _____ the singers.

    A. amung   B. among   C. ammung

16. Rhonda wanted to have a _____ show.

    A. puppet   B. pupet   C. pappet

17. Did you hear a _____ of the man?

    A. foutstep   B. footstap   C. footstep

Unit 12
Review lessons 7-11
Part 1

Circle the letter of the correct spelling for the word that belongs in the blank.

1. Your _____ is inside your skull.

    A. brian	B. brane	C. brain

2. The _____ tracks were close to their house.

    A. railroad	B. rialroad	C. railraod

3. Frankie had a _____ in his head.

    A. pane	B. pain	C. pian

4. A _____ can climb easily.

    A. monkey	B. mounkey	C. monkee

5. Some bees can make _____ .

    A. huney	B. honeey	C. honey

6. Do not _____ on thin ice.

    A. scate	B. skate	C. skaet

7. People were at the flea market before _____.

    A. daylite	B. daylight	C. daylighte

8. Finally the _____ of the sun began to shine.

    A. raise	B. rase	C. rays

9. I like to eat pork _____.

    A. steak   B. staek   C. stake

10. We should give the man a _____ .

    A. key   B. keye   C. keey

11. _____ seated while the van is moving.

    A. Remane   B. Remain   C. remian

12. I did not want the man to _____ the little chair.

    A. brake   B. braek   C. break

13. Parents should _____ their children in the right way.

    A. rays   B. raise   C. raize

14. Was the brown dog a _____?

    A. strae   B. straye   C. stray

15. I do not like for children to _____ lunches.

    A. trade   B. traed   C. tread

16. The children stood on the _____.

    A. staje   B. stage   C. stag

17. The _____ is very short.

    A. pony   B. poney   C. poony

18. Didn't you _____ who that guy was?

    A. kno   B. knoe   C. know

Unit 12
Review lessons 7-11
Part 2

Circle the letter of the correct spelling for the word that belongs in the blank.

1. You might get a ticket if you _____.

   A. spead   B. speed   C. spede

2. A pocket in a dress is a _____ thing to have.

   A. hande   B. handey   C. handy

3. A _____ drives a plane.

   A. pilot   B. pilet   C. pillot

4. _____ is a nice word to say when you ask for something.

   A. Please   B. Plaese   C. Pleese

5. We had a _____ birthday party for Donna and Kevin.

   A. shurprise   B. surpries   C. surprise

6. You can _____ the loaves of bread if you wish.

   A. frease   B. freeze   C. freaze

7. You can put _____ on your hands to make them soft.

   A. creem   B. cream   C. craem

8. Was the baby rabbit _____?

   A. alive   B. allive   C. alyve

9. What was your _____ when you were two years old?

    A. hieght   B. hite   C. height

10. The baby seems to have a _____ in his eyes when he smiles.

    A. gleam   B. gleem   C. gleme

11. Babies are _____ when they're first born.

    A. tinee   B. tiny   C. tiney

12. It is not good to act _____ while you're in church.

    A. sillee   B. sily   C. silly

13. Count the veins on a _____.

    A. leaf   B. leef   C. leav

14. It is fun to jump in a _____ of leaves.

    A. pille   B. piel   C. pile

15. Do you _____ with the mayor?

    A. agrea   B. agree   C. agrree

16. I wanted _____ on the whole wedding dress.

    A. lace   B. lase   C. lass

17. Have you ever seen an _____ fly?

    A. eagel   B. eagle   C. eegle

18. How good is your _____ without glasses?

    A. site   B. sight   C. sighte

Unit 12
Review lessons 7-11
Part 3

Circle the letter of the correct spelling for the word that belongs in the blank.

1. Playing the _____ can be very relaxing.

    A. piano   B. peano   C. pianno

2. We should listen to the tour _____ when we tour the Capitol.

    A. gide   B. guide   C. giude

3. Pencils, paper, and erasers are some of the _____ we need for school.

    A. suplies   B. supplys   C. supplies

4. Patti's biggest dog is _____.

    A. hugge   B. huje   C. huge

5. James got the wood because it was _____.

    A. oak   B. oke   C. oek

6. The time does not change _____.

    A. tonite   B. toonight   C. tonight

7. The Bible says to pray that your _____ would not be in the winter.

    A. flite   B. flight   C. fligght

8. _____ is an expensive metal.

    A. Goold   B. Gold   C. Gode

9. Lynn hit the _____ with the car and bent it.

    A. post   B. poste   C. posst

10. I could hear the _____ from the front porch.

    A. siren   B. sirene   C. sirren

11. The baby is very _____.

    A. qute   B. kute   C. cute

12. Be _____ when the baby is sleeping.

    A. queit   B. quiet   C. kwite

13. I felt like letting out a _____ after I had a bike wreck.

    A. grone   B. graon   C. groan

14. Alex _____ to me this morning.

    A. spoke   B. spoak   C. spoek

15. You can _____ your fingers when counting in math.

    A. usa   B. use   C. yous

16. I wish I was _____ to be the president.

    A. qalified   B. qualifyed   C. qualified

17. A teacher should never _____ a child.

    A. abuse   B. abuze   C. ubuse

Unit 12
Review lessons 7-11
Part 4

Circle the letter of the correct spelling for the word that belongs in the blank.

1. Sixteen ounces of water is one _____.

    A. pient   B. pint   C. pinte

2. Please practice your _____ on the piano.

    A. music   B. muzic   C. muisic

3. I am glad that I did not break a _____ when I fell.

    A. boan   B. bone   C. boen

4. Put your plate on the _____.

    A. table   B. taebl   C. tabel

5. We stayed in a _____ in Ohio.

    A. hoetel   B. hotell   C. hotel

6. Are you a _____ in this school?

    A. pupil   B. puepil   C. pupill

7. Do not sit _____ a tree limb during a storm.

    A. bellow   B. beloe   C. below

8. The tree _____ fall on you.

    A. mieht   B. might   C. mite

9. Are we ready for the _____?

    A. proegram   B. programe   C. program

10. Do not hold your _____ in front of your face.

    A. paper   B. paeper   C. papper

11. An _____ would be found in a desert.

    A. oaesis   B. oasis   C. oasise

12. I do not want you to fall _____ a cliff.

    A. over   B. ovur   C. overe

13. I want to sew the _____ in my dress.

    A. seame   B. seam   C. seem

14. An _____ might fall from a tree.

    A. akorn   B. accorn   C. acorn

15. You might _____ enjoy this program.

    A. evin   B. evven   C. even

16. How much _____ did Jimmy have in his bank?

    A. money   B. muney   C. monee

17. I hit my _____ against the door facing.

    A. elboa   B. elbow   C. ellbow

Unit 18
Review lessons 13-17
Part 1

Circle the letter of the correct spelling for the word that belongs in the blank.

1. Did we sing "We Wish You a _____ Christmas?"

    A. marry   B. mery   C. merry

2. You can find milk in the _____ section.

    A. dairy   B. derry   C. darry

3. Small children should not play with a _____.

    A. marbel   B. marble   C. marrble

4. I got that garment for a _____ price.

    A. barrgain   B. bargain   C. bargen

5. Many trees are _____ in the winter.

    A. bare   B. barre   C. bear

6. We should study to _____ for a test.

    A. perpare   B. prepair   C. prepare

7. A _____ has four sides that are all the same length.

    A. square   B. sqare   C. squair

8. The glass was _____.

    A. cleer   B. clear   C. klear

9. A _____ is a fruit.

    A. pare   B. pear   C. peer

10. You should never play _____.

    A. unfare   B. unfaer   C. unfair

11. Jean lived in the _____ house.

    A. rear   B. reer   C. raer

12. Walk _____ down the road.

    A. farrther   B. farthur   C. farther

13. God wants us to _____ with others.

    A. shair   B. share   C. sharre

14. Could Frankie go on an _____ for me?

    A. errand   B. arrand   C. erand

15. He may _____ to be tired.

    A. appeer   B. apear   C. appear

16. Is the _____ for the election of a president?

    A. yeer   B. year   C. yere

17. Running an obstacle _____ can be fun.

    A. course   B. corse   C. corese

18. To what _____ do you belong?

    A. cherch   B. charch   C. church

Unit 18
Review lessons 13-17
Part 2

Circle the letter of the correct spelling for the word that belongs in the blank.

1. We know that _____ can not really fly.

    A. reindear			B. reindeer			C. raindeer

2. Spelling is a very _____ thing to learn to do.

    A. impourtant		B. imporetant		C. important

3. Nothing means the same as _____.

    A. zeroe			B. zero				C. zeero

4. Try to memorize the books of the Bible in _____.

    A. order			B. oarder			C. ordur

5. Daniel Boone was a famous _____.

    A. pionear			B. pioneer			C. pineer

6. One guy was using an _____ to row the boat up the flooded street.

    A. oar				B. ore				C. orr

7. Many people try to spread good _____ at Christmas time.

    A. chear			B. cheere			C. cheer

8. It is not a normal thing for real people to just _____.

    A. disappear		B. dizappear		C. disapear

9. It hurts badly to get pricked by a _____.

   A. thoarn   B. thorne   C. thorn

10. The man tried to be a _____.

    A. hearo   B. hero   C. heroe

11. I do not want you to be _____ all the papers.

    A. tearing   B. teering   C. tering

12. I would like to have a deck on my house instead of this _____.

    A. proch   B. porech   C. porch

13. She cut the cloth with _____.

    A. sheers   B. sheres   C. shears

14. I do not play in _____ very much.

    A. sports   B. sporets   C. sporrts

15. You would be expected to shed a _____ if your mother died.

    A. teir   B. tear   C. tere

16. We should never _____ at anyone because they are slow at learning.

    A. jear   B. jeer   C. jeir

17. I was a _____ at the meeting.

    A. visitor   B. visiter   C. visitar

18. Kevin admitted they had made an _____.

    A. errer   B. eror   C. error

Unit 18
Review lessons 13-17
Part 3

Circle the letter of the correct spelling for the word that belongs in the blank.

1. Do not stay outside if a _____ begins.

    A. sterm   B. stoarm   C. storm

2. Go to a basement if there is to be a _____.

    A. tornado   B. torenado   C. tornadoe

3. High winds can cause things to _____ in the air.

    A. twerl   B. twirl   C. twirrl

4. The _____ is the top of a thing.

    A. surface   B. surfase   C. serface

5. One can make butter by using a _____.

    A. chern   B. churn   C. chrun

6. Brenda is a _____ woman.

    A. shorte   B. shoart   C. short

7. Zach has been a diligent _____ for his uncle.

    A. workur   B. worker   C. werker

8. I had _____ dollars.

    A. forteen   B. fourten   C. fourteen

9. Keep a _____ of all your stories.

    A. jernal   B. jornal   C. journal

10. Jimmy seemed to be _____ at my house.

    A. bored   B. board   C. borred

11. A _____ is a small donkey.

    A. burro   B. buro   C. burrow

12. Clarence received an _____ for his safety idea.

    A. awerd   B. awarrd   C. award

13. Anthony was the _____ child in the family.

    A. forth   B. fourth   C. foreth

14. The child's face was _____.

    A. derty   B. dirty   C. dirtie

15. Did you hear the _____ of a bird?

    A. chirp   B. churp   C. cherp

16. I have a _____ hanging by the computer.

    A. calender   B. calinder   C. calendar

17. Going to Florida is a long _____.

  A. jerney   B. journey
  C. joarney

Unit 18
Review lessons 13-17
Part 4

Circle the letter of the correct spelling for the word that belongs in the blank.

1. Spread _____ on the bread before it's put into the toaster oven.

    A. buter   B. butter   C. buttir

2. It might be fun to visit a _____ to see how vegetables are canned.

    A. cannery   B. canery   C. cannury

3. They ran to the _____ when the tornado was coming.

    A. cellar   B. cellur   C. celar

4. Benjamin seems to get _____ during the night.

    A. thursty   B. thirstie   C. thirsty

5. I had read _____ in the Bible last night than James had.

    A. furthir   B. furrther   C. further

6. Make sure you put a _____ at the end of all telling sentences.

    A. pereod   B. period   C. peariod

7. I like the _____ blue.

    A. color   B. collor   C. collur

8. James would _____ not eat coconut.

    A. ratther   B. rather   C. rathir

9. Donna began to _____ for Benjamin.

    A. serch   B. saerch   C. search

10. Some people _____ Walmart through the Exit door.

    A. inter   B. enter   C. ennter

11. Some people _____ blue more than red.

    A. favor   B. favoor   C. favur

12. _____ blocks before you leave school.

    A. Gather   B. Gathur   C. Gether

13. I would like to score _____ on the test than I did before.

    A. beter   B. better   C. bettir

14. Is this been a _____ day for us?

    A. regelar   B. reggular   C. regular

15. It doesn't _____ to me whether we eat at McDonalds or KFC.

    A. matter   B. mater   C. mattur

16. Make sure your _____ is down on your shirt.

    A. colar   B. coller   C. collar

17. I would like to _____ to play the piano better.

    A. leern   B. learn   C. lern

Unit 24
Review lessons 19-23
Part 1

Circle the letter of the correct spelling for the word that belongs in the blank.

1. Are you going to _____ the answer?

    A. gess   B. geuss   C. guess

2. Donna is Abigail's _____.

    A. aunt   B. ant   C. aunte

3. A little pig can _____.

    A. squeel   B. squeal   C squeil

4. I have some _____ material.

    A. scrapp   B. scrap   C. scrape

5. Frankie mowed the grass in the _____.

    A. field   B. feild   C. feald

6. Byron likes to _____ on the door.

    A. knok   B. knoke   C. knock

7. Put butter in the microwave to _____ it.

    A. sofen   B. soffen   C. soften

8. _____ an orange to get the juice from it.

    A. squaze   B. squeeze   C. squeese

9. If you lift weights, you cam make your muscles _____.

    A. strong   B. strung   C. stong

10. A rock _____ into the river.

    A. sannk   B. senk   C. sank

11. There was a cover on the door _____.

    A. nob   B. knobe   C. knob

12. Did you only eat a _____ of the cake?

    A. crumb   B. crume   C. crum

13. Is there a _____ in England now?

    A. quean   B. queen   C. quene

14. Please pull the van _____ into the driveway.

    A. streight   B. straight   C. strate

15. Sometimes a mother may _____ her child.

    A. scoeld   B. skold   C. scold

16. Right is the opposite of _____.

    A. wrong   B. rong   C. wronng

17. James attached the _____ to the building.

    A. sine   B. sien   C. sign

18. The _____ was yellow.

    A. skwash   B. squash   C. squosh

Unit 24
Review lessons 19-23
Part 2

Circle the letter of the correct spelling for the word that belongs in the blank.

1. It is _____ to see snow in Kentucky in July.

   A. strange   B. stranje   C. straenge

2. A wise man would not _____ his house on sand.

   A. bild   B. build   C. builed

3. I did not want one _____ to be left in the shirt.

   A. wrenkle   B. wrinkle   C. wrinkel

4. I would like to see the inside of the _____.

   A. castle   B. casle   C. castel

5. Two dimes and one nickel equal one _____.

   A. quartre   B. quarrter   C. quarter

6. Did the boys make Lillie _____?

   A. screme   B. scream   C. screem

7. I still have _____ in this pen.

   A. ingk   B. enk   C. ink

8. Please _____ the house while we are gone.

   A. gaurd   B. gard   C. guard

9. Did he smash his _____?

    A. thumb   B. thume   C. thum

10. Was Martha Washington a _____?

    A. squow   B. squaw   C. squau

11. Do you have a _____?

    A. skrapbook   B. scrapebook   C. scrapbook

12. Has Benjamin learned to _____ his right eye?

    A. wink   B. wingk   C. wingke

13. You can _____ down to pray.

    A. kneel   B. kneal   C. kneele

14. You could carry a _____ on your shoulders.

    A. laem   B. lame   C. lamb

15. To win you can not be a _____.

    A. quitter   B. quiter   C. quittor

16. A back _____ can be very painful.

    A. strane   B. straen   C. strain

17. It bothered William that he was almost _____.

    A. bold   B. bald   C. bauld

18. Was David _____?

    A. gilty   B. guilty   C. guiltty

Unit 24
Review lessons 19-23
Part 3

Circle the letter of the correct spelling for the word that belongs in the blank.

1. Where is my black _____?

   A. comeb   B. come   C. comb

2. I enjoy the _____ at our house.

   A. quietness   B. queitness   C. quietnees

3. Please _____ the stove.

   A. skrub   B. scrub   C. scrube

4. _____ the eggs together.

   A. Bleand   B. Blend   C. Blind

5. I do not want to be involved in a _____.

   A. wreck   B. wrreck   C. wrek

6. Children should _____ God and their parents.

   A. honer   B. hounor   C. honor

7. Two-year-old children like to _____.

   A. squerm   B. squorm   C. squirm

8. Lee likes to _____ the drums with the drumsticks.

   A. strike   B. strik   C. strick

9. Kevin used to _____ his teeth together at night.

    A. griend   B. grind   C. grinde

10. Please _____ a letter to Charles.

    A. wriet   B. writte   C. write

11. I _____ some shirts last week.

    A. boght   B. bought   C. bout

12. It is not nice to _____ with people.

    A. quarel   B. quarrel   C. quarrle

13. Will you _____ my back?

    A. scratch   B. skratch   C. scrach

14. We should stay busy to exercise our _____.

    A. mind   B. miend   C. minde

15. Patti wore a brace on her _____.

    A. wriste   B. wrisst   C. wrist

16. Do you want a _____ bird for a pet?

    A. wield   B. wild   C. willd

17. What kind of _____ did the woman ask?

    A. question   B. queschion   C. questoin

Unit 24
Review lessons 19-23
Part 4

Circle the letter of the correct spelling for the word that belongs in the blank.

1. He pulled the truck out of the ditch with a thick _____.

    A. strrap   B. strap   C. strapp

2. There was a _____ of dirt on the grave.

    A. mound   B. mownd   C. moud

3. My _____ was hurting.

    A. knae   B. knea   C. knee

4. I do not talk to the mayor very _____.

    A. offen   B. often   C. offten

5. Monica was _____ to stand up.

    A. quieck   B. quick   C. quik

6. You could walk in a _____.

    A. stream   B. streem   C. straem

7. Do not _____ your eyes when getting a picture taken.

    A. blenk   B. blingk   C. blink

8. Mr. Poindexter was a _____ at our church.

    A. gest   B. guest   C. geust

9. Can you _____ a tune?

    A. whistel   B. wistle   C. whistle

10. I saw a _____ in our yard.

    A. squirrel   B. squirel   C. squirrle

11. Was there plenty of _____ to go around her waist?

    A. streng   B. sttring   C. string

12. I do not want Frankie to be _____.

    A. blind   B. blinde   C. blinnd

13. Would you want to play a _____?

    A. giutar   B. guitar   C. guiter

14. Please _____ for directions.

    A. lisen   B. listen   C. lissten

15. I did not like to hear Noah's desk _____.

    A. squeek   B. sqeak   C. squeak

16. Please fasten some _____ on the window.

    A. screan   B. screne   C. screen

17. Choose the correct word for each _____.

    A. blank   B. blink   C. blenk

Unit 30
Review lessons 25-29
Part 1

Circle the letter of the correct spelling for the word that belongs in the blank.

1. Have you ever seen one _____ flying alone?

    A. gouse   B. guse   C. goose

2. The twin girls were two little _____.

    A. beauties   B. bueties   C. beautys

3. I _____ kickball with the boys.

    A. plaeyd   B. playd   C. played

4. I have _____ to try to live right.

    A. desided   B. decided   C. decideed

5. Please do not see who make me the _____!

    A. madest   B. maddest   C. maddist

6. James had all of his _____ pulled.

    A. teeth   B. teath   C. tethe

7. There are many _____ in the reading books.

    A. storyes   B. storys   C. stories

8. I had been _____ worksheets for a long time.

    A. copying   B. copeing   C. coppying

9. Who was _____ Zach when he ran into the table?

    A. chaseing   B. chasing   C. chaesing

10. Who has seen the _____ bat in Louisville?

    A. largeest   B. largest   C. larjest

11. The picture showed three _____.

    A. calves   B. calfs   C. calfes

12. I saw two _____ in the lot.

    A. ponys   B. ponnies   C. ponies

13. James _____ Jimmy on his shoulders.

    A. carryed   B. caried   C. carried

14. I made a heart-_____ cake.

    A. shaped   B. shapped   C. shapeed

15. The big blue van was the _____ vehicle we had ever owned.

    A. finnest   B. finest   C. finst

16. I had two _____.

    A. childrun   B. children   C. chiledren

17. The woman had two _____.

    A. babbies   B. babys   C. babies

18. Kevin and Patti got _____ in September.

    A. married   B. marryed   C. marrid

Unit 30
Review lessons 25-29
Part 2

Circle the letter of the correct spelling for the word that belongs in the blank.

1. Had you _____ the decorations?

    A. notised   B. noticed   C. noticeed

2. David was the _____ of all the people in Israel.

    A. bravest   B. bravst   C. bravvest

3. Would you like to write the story of my _____?

    A. liffe   B. life   C. live

4. How many _____ did we see at the zoo?

    A. monkeeys   B. monkeyes   C. monkeys

5. I _____ eating chicken at the restaurant.

    A. injoyed   B. enjoyd   C. enjoyed

6. I was _____ myself to finish the work before going to bed.

    A. forcing   B. forsing   C. forceing

7. Which pig was the _____?

    A. fatest   B. fattest   C. fattist

8. Myrna had one _____.

    A. child   B. childe   C. chield

9. How many more _____ could we tolerate and still be on time?

    A. delaiys   B. delayes   C. delays

10. I _____ more papers for Dale.

    A. copyed   B. copied   C. coppied

11. Are they still _____ when they will allow you to work?

    A. deciding   B. desiding   C. decideing

12. This lamp is _____ than the one in the bedroom.

    A. largir   B. largor   C. larger

13. James bought a bunch of _____ at the thrift store.

    A. knifes   B. knives   C. kniffs

14. Fifty _____ equals the same as two quarters.

    A. penies   B. pennys   C. pennies

15. Kevin and I were _____ kickball with Jimmy and David.

    A. playing   B. plaieing   C. playeng

16. The boys were _____ in the parking lot.

    A. racing   B. raceing   C. rasing

17. That is the _____ church in Louisville.

    A. begest   B. biggist   C. biggest

18. Many _____ fly south for the winter.

    A. gease   B. geese   C. geece

Unit 30
Review lessons 25-29
Part 3

Circle the letter of the correct spelling for the word that belongs in the blank.

1. I sold some _____ at the flea market.

    A. trays   B. trayes   C. trais

2. Robert was _____ James's sister.

    A. marying   B. marrying   C. merrying

3. David kept _____ the paper to make the shape of a boat.

    A. creasing   B. creaseing   C. cresing

4. Who is the _____ teacher you have ever known?

    A. nisest   B. niceest   C. nicest

5. Did one of Donna's cows have a _____?

    A. caff   B. calfe   C. calf

6. James likes to read the _____ in the newspaper.

    A. funies   B. funnies   C. funnys

7. Charles was finally _____ to my question.

    A. replying   B. replieing   C. replyeng

8. I was _____ Ben's cute little smile.

    A. noticeing   B. noticing   C. noticeng

9. Darien did a _____ job making rolls than most students.

    A. finner   B. finor   C. finer

10. Does Abigail have a _____ now?

    A. tooth   B. touth   C. toothe

11. I have plenty of _____ at my house.

    A. toyss   B. toyes   C. toys

12. Monica _____ here for one day.

    A. stayd   B. stayed   C. staeyd

13. Isaiah _____ Katie often when they were playing hide-and-seek.

    A. chassed   B. chaesd   C. chased

14. Robbie is _____ than I am when dealing with snakes.

    A. braever   B. braver   C. bravver

15. Donna cut the watermelon with a sharp _____.

    A. knif   B. knife   C. knief

16. Were you counting the _____ as you went down the highway?

    A. valleys   B. valeys   C. valleyes

17. Patti _____ to my message.

    A. replid   B. replyed   C. replied

Unit 30
Review lessons 25-29
Part 4

Circle the letter of the correct spelling for the word that belongs in the blank.

1. Frankie _____ to see if he could cross the track before the train was there.

    A. raceed   B. raced   C. rased

2. Byron is _____ than Abigail.

    A. biger   B. bigger   C. biggor

3. Beverly was a _____ who worked with us for the election.

    A. woeman   B. woman   C. women

4. Riding _____ was a common form of travel many years ago.

    A. donkeyes   B. dongkeys   C. donkeys

5. How long will you be _____ with us?

    A. steying   B. stayeng   C. staying

6. Make sure your paper does not get _____.

    A. creased   B. cresed   C. creassed

7. I tried to be _____ than I had been the other time.

    A. niser   B. nicer   C. niccer

8. Many _____ were lost in the Vietnam War.

    A. lives   B. lifes   C. liffes

9. There are seven _____ in a week.

    A. dayes   B. daze   C. days

10. Kevin was not _____ Byron when we saw him Tuesday.

    A. carrying   B. carying   C. careying

11. Some police officers might feel _____ to act mean.

    A. forsed   B. forced   C. forceed

12. I am much _____ than I was ten years ago.

    A. fater   B. fateer   C. fatter

13. Three _____ worked in our precinct in May 2012.

    A. woman   B. women   C. wimen

14. We went to two _____ one day before we checked out any books.

    A. libraries   B. libraires   C. librarries

15. We were _____ the preaching of Bro. Randy Webb.

    A. enjoing   B. enjoying   C. enjoyeng

16. You can be _____ the clay into balls.

    A. shapping   B. shapeing   C. shaping

17. The principal seemed to be _____ than most of the teachers that were there.

    A. madder   B. maddor   C. mader

Unit 36
Review lessons 31-35
Part 1

Circle the letter of the correct spelling for the word that belongs in the blank.

1. _____ the value of the jeep?

    A. Whot's	B. What's	C. Whats

2. It is _____ to drink alcohol.

    A. needless	B. nedless	C. needles

3. I'm glad I did not _____ to America on the Mayflower.

    A. sale	B. sael	C. sail

4. Toddlers can easily cause people to _____.

    A. laugh	B. lauph	C. laff

5. We had an _____ vacation.

    A. enjoyabel	B. injoyable	C. enjoyable

6. _____ you tune the piano?

    A. How'ed	B. Hou'd	C. How'd

7. The story of Cinderella is a _____.

    A. tale	B. tail	C. tele

8. Please call me on the _____.

    A. talephone	B. telephone	C. telefone

9. It would _____ me for a close friend to die.

    A. sadden   B. saden   C. saddin

10. It is _____ in the school on Saturdays.

    A. peaseful   B. peacful   C. peaceful

11. _____ been making good grades.

    A. Sh'ed   B. She'd   C. She'hd

12. It is not a good feeling for your voice to be _____.

    A. horse   B. hoarse   C. hoarce

13. Have you seen a _____ jump out of the water?

    A. dollphin   B. dolfin   C. dolphin

14. There was a big _____ in the school.

    A. disturbance   B. disturbence   C. disterbance

15. The small flashlight gave a lot of light in the _____.

    A. darkness   B. darknes   C. darkess

16. He knew _____ take care of the children.

    A. thay'd   B. they'd   C. they'ld

17. Donna has three _____ children.

    A. mail   B. mael   C. male

18. The sandpaper was _____.

    A. rough   B. rouph   C. ruff

Unit 36
Review lessons 31-35
Part 2

Circle the letter of the correct spelling for the word that belongs in the blank.

1. How much does a _____ stamp costs?

    A. posttage   B. postege   C. postage

2. God's _____ to us is so great!

    A. goodniss   B. goodness   C. goodnese

3. _____ be going somewhere soon.

    A. We'll   B. Wi'll   C. We'l

4. _____ you please be quiet?

    A. Wood   B. Would   C. Wuold

5. Write a _____ on how birds fly.

    A. paragraph   B. paragragh   C. paregraph

6. Did she pay the _____ bill?

    A. insurance   B. inshurance   C. insurence

7. Did you see the farm _____ in the parade?

    A. eqipment   B. equipmant   C. equipment

8. _____ living in the house?

    A. Who'is   B. Who's   C. Whose

9. James got the _____ out of the box.

    A. male   B. maile   C. mail

10. People can learn to read if they use _____.

    A. phonics   B. fonics   C. ponics

11. We should eat a _____ diet.

    A. wholsome   B. wholesum   C. wholesome

12. I've already paid the _____.

    A. paiment   B. payment   C. paymint

13. _____ not come to school on Saturday.

    A. Sh'el   B. She'll   C. She'l

14. I saw a dog with a short _____.

    A. tail   B. tale   C. tell

15. Kenny is Victoria's _____.

    A. nefew   B. nepheu   C. nephew

16. Frankie read the _____ from the Bible.

    A. passege   B. passage   C. pasage

17. Tuning that piano seemed _____.

    A. hopeluss   B. hopless   C. hopeless

18. Because he was sick, Jimmy did not have a _____ night.

    A. restful   B. resful   C. restfull

Unit 36
Review lessons 31-35
Part 3

Circle the letter of the correct spelling for the word that belongs in the blank.

1. _____ want to graduate some day.

    A. They'll B. Thay'll C. The'yll

2. _____ want to go home with me?

    A. Whu'd B. Who'd C. Wh'od

3. Have you ever tasted of a _____?

    A. beet B. beat C. bete

4. Bruce said he was an _____.

    A. orfan B. orpan C. orphan

5. The answer was _____.

    A. aceptable B. acceptabel C. acceptable

6. I would like to have _____ candy.

    A. sum B. some C. sume

7. Do you have _____ money to buy a watch?

    A. enouf B. enough C. enouph

8. Greg could be of _____ to me.

    A. assistance B. asistance C. assistence

9. The carpet was not _____.

    A. spotlass   B. spottless   C. spotless

10. _____ have some money if you would get a job.

    A. Yo'd   B. You'd   C. You'ld

11. Earl got some of the _____.

    A. would   B. wood   C. wuold

12. Wendy wanted me to have a _____ of her.

    A. foto   B. photoe   C. photo

13. We packed a lot of _____ for the trip.

    A. baggage   B. bagage   C. baggege

14. I am _____ for my health.

    A. thinkful   B. thankful   C. thankfull

15. That piano _____ sound like it's in tune.

    A. doezn't   B. dusn't   C. doesn't

16. Can you get the right _____ on the drums?

    A. beat   B. beet   C. bete

17. Do you have a bad _____?

    A. coff   B. cough   C. couph

Unit 36
Review lessons 31-35
Part 4

Circle the letter of the correct spelling for the word that belongs in the blank.

1. What kind of _____ did he make during the debate?

    A. statment   B. statement   C. statemint

2. Was thee a _____ of water during the summer?

    A. shortege   B. shortaje   C. shortage

3. _____ stay home for a while.

    A. He'ld   B. Hed   C. He'd

4. I do not own a _____.

    A. horse   B. hoarse   C. horsse

5. The tangerine peel was _____.

    A. tuff   B. tough   C. touph

6. I was _____ to work Friday.

    A. available   B. availeable   C. availabel

7. Brenda's _____ made me enjoy working there.

    A. kindless   B. kindness   C. kindeness

8. I wish _____ learned to play the piano better.

    A. Id   B. I'ld   C. I'd

9. The house was for _____.

    A. sale   B. sail   C. sell

10. "No pain, no gain" is a famous _____.

    A. frase   B. phraze   C. phrase

11. James made a _____ doll house.

    A. woodan   B. wooden   C. wouden

12. We should be _____ when climbing a ladder.

    A. carful   B. careful   C. carefull

13. _____ we living in the United States?

    A. Aren't   B. Aren'ot   C. Arn't

14. Fifteen is the _____ of ten plus five.

    A. sum   B. some   C. sume

15. Running at five miles per hour can be _____.

    A. tirsome   B. tiresum   C. tiresome

16. This book is more than a _____.

    A. pamflet   B. pamphlet   C. pamphlit

17. Because God is so good to us, we should be _____.

    A. cherful   B. cheerful   C. chearful

Answer Key
Unit 1

Page 5
A. 1. crack   2. damp   B. 1. every   2. never
   3. animal   4. travel   3. address   4. pest
   5. camel   6. planet   5. pepper   6. mend
   7. grand   8. address   7. lemon

C. 1. a   2. a e   3. a   4. a i a
   5. a e   6. e   7. e   8. e e
   9. e   10. a e   11. e   12. e e
  13. a e   14. a

Page 6
A. 1. pepper   2. never   B. 1. noun   2. adjective
   3. planet   4. crack   3. verb   4. noun
   5. animal   6. every   5. adjective 6. noun

C. 1. travel   2. never   3. camel
   4. address   5. damp   6. mend

Page 7
1. camel   2. animal   3. pest
4. travel   5. planet   6. damp
7. never   8. lemon   9. cracked
10. every   11. pepper   12. grand
13. address   14. mend

Unit 2

Page 12
A. 1. mist 2. rich
3. sink 4. silk
5. mittens

B. 1. socks 2. robin
3. doctor 4. topcoat
5. copper

C. 1. undone 2. bunch
3. strum 4. rumble

D. 1. silk 2. socks
3. mittens 4. rumble

E. 1. u o   2. o e   3. o o   4. o oa

Page 13
A. 1. sink 2. robin
3. doctor 4. rumble

B. 1. rich 2. undone

C. 1. mit-tens 2. un-done 3. rum-ble 4. rob-in
5. doc-tor 6. top-coat 7. cop-per

Page 14
1. mittens   socks   topcoat
2. doctor
3. mist
4. bunch
5. copper
6. silk
7. undone
8. robin
9. rich
10. rumble
11. sink

293

Unit 3

Page 19

A. 1. cabin 2. ladder
3. basket

B. 1. liver 2. chicken
3. similar

C. 1. stock 2. pocket

D. 1. tennis 2. empty
3. leather

E. 1. hundred 2. puppet
3. summer

F. 1. tennis 2. ladder
3. puppet 4. summer

Page 20

A. 1. noun 2. noun
3. noun 4. noun

B. 1. tennis 2. leather
3. stock

C. 1. lad-der 2. bas-ket 3. sum-mer 4. sim-i-lar
5. emp-ty 6. pup-pet 7. hun-dred

Page 21

1. Summer 2. chicken liver 3. basket
4. tennis 5. cabin 6. pocket
7. puppets 8. Stock 9. hundred
10. ladder 11. leather 12. empty
13. similar

Unit 4

Page 26

A. 1. plural   2. put   B. 1. oo   2. oo
    3. full   3. oo   4. ou

C. 1. shook   2. brook   D. 1. plural   2. footstep
    3. took   4. book   2. woodchuck   4. childhood

E. 1. brook   2. woodchuck   3. book

Page 27

A. 1. adjective   2. noun   3. verb   4. noun
    5. adjective   6. verb

B. 1. hood   plural   took
    2. brook   childhood   shook
    3. foot   put   wool
    4. book   full   took
    5. shook   took   woodchuck
    6. footstep   plural   should

Page 28

A. 1. brook   2. plural   3. shook
    4. childhood   5. footstep   6. woodchuck

B. 1. put   2. hood   3. full
    4. wool   5. book   6. Should
    7. took   8. foot

Unit 5

Page 33

A. 1. away 2. among B. 1. eleven 2. silent
   3. across 4. garage   3. celery 4. parent
                            5. number 6. oven

C. 1. pencil 2. family D. wagon

E. 1. eleven 2. celery 3. family

F. 1. u   2. o   3. i   4. e   5. e   6. e

Page 34

A. 1. number 2. parent B. 1. silent 2. wagon
   3. celery 4. careful   3. number
   5. away   6. family

C. 1. among   2. eleven 3. across
   4. oven   5. careful

Page 35

A. 1. pencil 2. eleven 3. parent
   4. family 5. garage 6. silent

B. 1 oven   2. celery 3. across
   4. away   5. wagon   6. number
   7. careful 8. among

Spelling Review 6- 4th grade
(answers)

Part 1	Part 2	Part 3	Part 4
1. A	1. C	1. B	1. C
2. C	2. A	2. A	2. A
3. B	3. B	3. A	3. B
4. B	4. A	4. C	4. B
5. A	5. B	5. B	5. A
6. C	6. C	6. B	6. C
7. B	7. C	7. C	7. A
8. C	8. A	8. A	8. C
9. C	9. B	9. C	9. C
10. A	10. A	10. C	10. B
11. A	11. C	11. B	11. A
12. B	12. B	12. B	12. A
13. C	13. B	13. A	13. B
14. B	14. A	14. C	14. C
15. C	15. C	15. B	15. B
16. B	16. B	16. A	16. A
17. A	17. A	17. C	17. C
18. C	18. B		

Unit 7

Page 41
A. 1. skate 2. trade B. 1. daylight 2. stray
   3. stage 4. lace   3. rays

C. 1. brain 2. railroad D. 1. steak 2. break
   3. remain 4. raise
   5. pain

E. 1. ai   2. ea   3. ay i   4. ai e
   5. ea   6. a e   7. ai oa   8. a e

Page 42
A. 1. re-main   2. day-light   3. rail-road

B. 1. raise   2. break   3. steak   4. pain

C. 1. trade   2. skate   3. daylight
   4. stage   5. stray   6. lace

Page 43
A. 1. remain   2. pain   3. brain
   4. rays   5. stray 6. daylight
   7. break   8. skate 9. lace
   10. trade   11. raise 12. stage
   13. railroad 14. steak

Unit 8

Page 48
A. 1. freeze 2. agree B. 1. leaf 2. gleam
   3. speed   3. please 4. cream

C. 1. honey 2. money D. 1. handy 2. silly
   3. key   4. monkey   3. pony

E. 1. o ey   2. ea   3. o   ey   4. a   ee   5. ee e
   6. o ey   7. ea e 8. ea   9. a   y   10. i y

Page 49
A. 1. gleam   2. silly   3. cream
   4. agree   5. please   6. monkey
   7. speed

B. 1. pony   2. freeze   3. honey
   4. money   5. leaf

C. Answers may vary.

Page 50
A. 1. honey   2. monkeys   3. speed
   4. silly   5. agree   6. pony
   7. money   8. freeze   9. cream
   10. leaf   11. key   12. gleam
   13. Please 14. handy

Unit 9

Page 55
A. 1. pile 2. surprise B. 1. sight 2. flight
   3. alive 4. guide   3. tonight

C. 1. pilot 2. tiny   D. 1. supplies 2. qualified
   3. siren 4. quiet

E. height

F. 1. i e 2. ie 3. ie
   4. i e 5. i   6. ei

Page 56
A. 1. pi-lot   2. sur-prise   3. a-live
   4. ti-ny   5. to-night   6. si-ren
   7. qui-et   8. sup-plies   9. qual-i-fied

B. 1. flight 2. guide 3. height 4. qualified 5. quiet
   6. sight   7. siren 8. surprise 9. tiny   10. tonight

Page 57
A. 1. heights   2. pilot   3. supplies
   4. guide   5. sight   6. flights
   7. quiet   8. surprise   9. pile
   10. alive   11. siren   12. qualified
   13. tiny   14. tonight

Unit 10

Page 62

A. 1. spoke 2. bone B. 1. groan 2. oak

C. 1. know 2. below D. 1. piano 2. gold
   3. siren 4. quiet   3. post 4. over

E. 1. huge 2. cute
   3. use 4. abuse

F. 1. post 2. gold
   3. cute 4. groan

Page 63

A. 1. over 2. bone 3. groan 4. oak
   5. below 6. spoke 7. gold 8. post

B. 1. huge 2. know 3. piano
   4. cute 5. use 6. abuse

C. 1. noun 2. adverb 3. verb
   4. adverb 5. verb 6. noun

Page 64

A. 1. cute 2. piano 3. huge
   4. over 5. spoke 6. abuse
   7. bone 8. know 9. post
   10. below 11. groaned 12. gold
   13. Use 14. Oak

Unit 11

Page 69
A. 1. acorn 2. table B. 1. even 2. seam
   3. paper 4. oasis   3. eagle

C. 1. program 2. oasis D. 1. might 2. pint
   3. hotel   4. elbow

E. 1. pupil 2. music

F. oasis

G. 1. might 2. pint
   3. seam

Page 70
A. 1. seam   2. oasis   3. even
   4. pint   5. pupil   6. might

B. 1. el-bow 2. a-corn 3. ho-tel
   4. pa-per 5. ea-gle 6. e-ven
   7. ta-ble 8. mu-sic 9. pro-gram

C. 1. pupil 2. might   3. music
   4. paper 5. elbow

Page 71
1. pupil   2. even   3. program 4. table
5. paper   6. music   7. might   8. hotel

1. oasis   2. acorn   3. eagle
4. pint   5. elbow   6. seam

302

Spelling Review 12- 4th grade
(answers)

Part 1	Part 2	Part 3	Part 4
1. C	1. B	1. A	1. B
2. A	2. C	2. B	2. A
3. B	3. A	3. C	3. B
4. A	4. A	4. C	4. A
5. C	5. C	5. A	5. C
6. B	6. B	6. C	6. A
7. B	7. B	7. B	7. C
8. C	8. A	8. B	8. B
9. A	9. C	9. A	9. C
10. A	10. A	10. A	10. A
11. B	11. B	11. C	11. B
12. C	12. C	12. B	12. A
13. B	13. A	13. C	13. B
14. C	14. C	14. A	14. C
15. A	15. B	15. B	15. C
16. B	16. A	16. C	16. A
17. A	17. B	17. A	17. B
18. C	18. B		

Unit 13

Page 77
A. 1. bargain   2. farther   B. 1. merry   2. errand
   3. marble   3. error

C. 1. pear   2. tearing   D. 1. unfair   2. dairy

E. 1. bare   2. square
   3. prepare   4. share

F. 1. pear   2. bare

Page 78
A. 1. bar′ gain   2. un-fair′   3. far′ ther
   4. dair′ y   5. er′ rand   6. mer′ ry
   7. pre pare′   8. mar′ ble   9. er′ ror
   10. tear′ ing

B. 1. bare   2. pear   3. square
   4. share   5. error   6. errand

Page 79
1. bargains   2. error   3. dairy   4. farther
5. tearing   6. bare   7. pear   8. marble
9. errand   10. prepare   11. unfair   12. square
13. share   14. Merry

Unit 14

Page 84
A. 1. rear　　2. clear　　　　B. 1. cheer　　2. reindeer
　3. appear　4. shears　　　　　3. pioneer　4. jeer
　5. disappear　6. year
　7. tear

C. 1. zero　　2. hero　　　　D. period

E. disappear

F. reindeer

Page 85
A. 1. zero　　　2. appear　　3. hero
　4. year　　　5. tear　　　6. clear
　7. pioneer　8. period

B. 1. zero　　　2. jeer　　　3. cheer
　4. shears　　5. reindeer

Page 86
1. pioneer　　2. period　　3. rear　　　4. zero
5. cheer　　　6. reindeer　7. appear　　8. years
9. disappeared　10. clear　11. shears　　12. hero
13. jeer　　　14. tears

Unit 15

Page 91
A. 1. thorn 2. sports B. 1. course 2. fourth
   3. order 4. porch   3. fourteen
   5. important 6. storm
   7. tornado 8. bored
   9. short

C. 1. oar   D. award

E. 1. important 2. tornado

F. 1. order 2. fourteen 3. award

Page 92
A. 1. storm noun   2. fourth adjective
   3. porch noun   4. important adjective

B. 1. fourteen 2. tornado   3. order 4. course
   5. oar   6. bored   7. thorn 8. sports
   9. short   10. award

Page 93
1. storm   2. important   3. award   4. porch
5. short   6. sports   7. course   8. thorns
9. order   10. fourth   11. tornado   12. oar
13. bored   14. fourteen

Unit 16

Page 98
A. 1. twirl   2. chirp   B. 1. churn   2. surface
   3. dirty   4. thirsty   3. burro   4. further
                5. church

C. 1. worker   D. 1. search   2. learn

E. 1. journal   2. journey

F. 1. ur   2. ear   3. our
   4. ir   5. or   6. ir

Page 99
A. 1. dirty   2. journey   3. twirl   4. worker
   5. further   6. thirsty   7. journal

B. 1. stir   2. churn   3. learn   4. search

C. 1. burro   2. chirp   3. church
   4. surface   5. twirl   6. worker

Page 100
1. surface   2. search   3. twirl   4. burro
5. learn   6. churn   7. thirsty   8. dirty
9. worker   10. further   11. chirp   12. journal
13. church   14. journey

307

Unit 17

Page 105
A. 1. gather 2. rather
3. cannery 4. better
5. enter 6. butter
7. matter

B. 1. regular 2. cellar
3. collar 4. calendar

C. 1. favor 2. color
3. visitor

D. 1. regular 2. cannery
3. calendar 4. visitor

E. 1. favor 2. gather 3. matter 4. butter

Page 106
A. calendar

B. 1. cannery 2. matter 3. favor 4. visitor

C. 1. gather 2. better 3. enter

D. 1. butter 2. collar 3. color
4. gather 5. rather 6. regular

Page 107
1. enter 2. color 3. better 4. calendar
5. rather 6. visitor 7. matter 8. cellar
9. cannery 10. favor 11. collar 12. Gather
13. regular 14. butter

Spelling Review 18- 4th grade
(answers)

Part 1	Part 2	Part 3	Part 4
1. C	1. B	1. C	1. B
2. A	2. C	2. A	2. A
3. B	3. B	3. B	3. A
4. B	4. A	4. A	4. C
5. A	5. B	5. B	5. C
6. C	6. A	6. C	6. B
7. A	7. C	7. B	7. A
8. B	8. A	8. C	8. B
9. B	9. C	9. C	9. C
10. C	10. B	10. A	10. B
11. A	11. A	11. A	11. A
12. C	12. C	12. C	12. A
13. B	13. C	13. B	13. B
14. A	14. A	14. B	14. C
15. C	15. B	15. A	15. A
16. B	16. B	16. C	16. C
17. A	17. A	17. B	17. B
18. C	18. C		

Unit 19

Page 113
A. 1. knock 2. knob
3. knee 4. kneel

B. 1. wrong 2. write
3. wrinkle 4. wreck
5. wrist

C. 1. guess 2. guest
3. guard 4. guitar
5. guilty

D. 1. knock 2. write
3. guest 4. guard
5. kneel 6. wrong

E. 1. wrinkle 2. guitar 3. guilty

Page 114
A. 1. knee, kneel 2. knock, knob
3. write, wrinkle, wrist 4. guard, guess, guest

B. 1. guilty 2. guitar 3. wrong 4. knob

C. 1. guilty 2. wrong

D. 1. guilt-y 2. gui-tar

Page 115
A. 1. guitar 2. knee 3. write 4. wrong
5. guard 6. wrist 7. knock 8. guess
9. guilty 10. guest

B. 1. wreck 2. kneel 3. wrinkle 4. knob

Unit 20

Page 120
A. 1. thumb   2. lamb   B. 1. bought   2. sign
   3. crumb 4. comb

C. 1. often   2. castle   D. 1. aunt   2. bought
   3. soften 4. whistle   3. build
   5. listen

E. 1. bought 2. honor

F. 1. aunt   2. bought   3. sign   4. comb

Page 121
A. 1. build   2. crumb   3. aunt   4. comb
   5. castle 6. thumb   7. whistle 8. often
   9. lamb   10. soften 11. sign   12. bought
  13. honor 14. listen

B. 1. of-ten 2. cas-tle   3. soft-en
   4. hon-or 5. whis-tle 6. lis-ten

C. 1. aunt   2. lamb   3. castle

Page 122
A. 1. thumb   2. aunt   3. often   4. comb
   5. castle 6. sign   7. honor   8. crumb
   9. whistle

B. 1. soften 2. bought   3. listen
   4. lamb   5. build

311

Unit 21

Page 127
A. 1. squirrel 2. squirm
   3. squash 4. squeal
   5. squeeze 6. squeak
   7. squaw

B. 1. queen 2. quietness
   3. quarter 4. question
   5. quarrel 6. quick
   7. quitter

C. 1. quarter 2. question
   3. quarrel 4. quitter
   5. squirrel

D. 1. quietness

E. 1. quarter 2. quick

Page 128
A. 1. quarrel 2. quarter 3. queen 4. question 5. quietness

B. 1. squash 2. squaw 3. squeal 4. squirm 5. squirrel

C. 1. quick 2. quitter 3. squeeze 4. squeak

D. 1. qui-et-ness 2. quar-ter 3. ques-tion
   4. quar-rel 5. squir-rel

Page 129
A. 1. squash 2. Queen 3. squirrel 4. quarrel
   5. question 6. squeeze 7. squaw 8. squeal
   9. squirm 10. quick 11. quietness 12. quarter
   13. squeak 14. quitter

B. 1. soften 2. bought 3. listen
   4. lamb 5. build

312

Unit 22

Page 134
A. 1. strange 2. strain   B. 1. scrap 2. scratch
   3. strap   4. stream   3. scrub 4. scream
   5. straight 6. string   5. screen 6. scrapbook
   7. strike   8. strong

C. 1. strain   2. straight   D. scrapbook
   3. stream scream 4. strange

E. 1. strong   2. strange

Page 135
A. 1. strange   2. stream   3. string
   1. scrap   2. screen   3. scrub
   1. straight 2. strain   3. strap

B. 1. scratch   2. scream   3. strike

C. 1. scrapbook 2. straight

Page 136
A. 1. scratch   2. screen   3. strange   4. straight
   5. scrapbook   6. scrub   7. scrap   8. strap
   9. scream   10. strain   11. strong   12. strike
   13. stream   14. string

Unit 23

Page 141

A. 1. scold 2. field B. 1. mind 2. mound
   3. wild   4. bald   3. blind 4. grind
                         5. blend

C. 1. wink 2. blink D. 1. scold 2. blink
   3. ink   4. sank   3. blind 4. grind
   5. blank   5. blank 6. blend

E. 1. old

F. 1. wink 2. blink

Page 142

A. 1. mound 2. ink   3. scold 4. blink
   5. bald   6. blank 7. wild

B. 1. field 2. mind   3. wink
   4. grind 5. sank

C. 1. blind 2. blend

Page 143

A. 1. blind 2. mound 3. field 4. mind
   5. blink 6. scold 7. wild

B. 1. sank   2. wink   3. ink   4. bald
   5. blank 6. blend 7. grind

314

Spelling Review 24- 4th grade
(answers)

Part 1	Part 2	Part 3	Part 4
1. C	1. A	1. C	1. B
2. A	2. B	2. A	2. A
3. B	3. B	3. B	3. C
4. B	4. A	4. B	4. B
5. A	5. C	5. A	5. B
6. C	6. B	6. C	6. A
7. C	7. C	7. C	7. C
8. B	8. C	8. A	8. B
9. A	9. A	9. B	9. C
10. C	10. B	10. C	10. A
11. C	11. C	11. B	11. C
12. A	12. A	12. B	12. A
13. B	13. A	13. A	13. B
14. B	14. C	14. A	14. B
15. C	15. A	15. C	15. C
16. A	16. C	16. B	16. C
17. C	17. B	17. A	17. A
18. B	18. B		

Unit 25

Page 149
A. 1. lives   2. calves   B. 1. geese   2. teeth
   3. knives   3. women   4. children

C. 1. goose   2. tooth   D. 1. knife   2. knives
   3. geese   4. teeth

E. 1. calf   2. life   3. knife

Page 150
A. 1. calf   2. geese   3. lives
   4. woman   5. knives   6. tooth

B. 1. calves   2. goose   3. knife
   4. teeth   5. child   6. life

C. 1. wom-en   2. chil-dren

D. 1. life   2. lives   3. knife   4. knives

Page 151
A. 1. women   2. woman   3. tooth   4. teeth
   5. knife   6. knives   7. child   8. children
   9. goose   10. geese   11. life   12. lives
   13. calf   14. calves

Unit 26

Page 156

A. 1. beauties 2. ponies B. 1. valleys 2. donkeys
3. pennies 4. babies 3. monkeys 4. delays
5. funnies 6. stories 5. days 6. toys
7. libraries 7. trays

C. 1. stories 2. beauties D. 1. toys 2. funnies
3. libraries 4. babies
5. donkeys

Page 157

A. 1. pennies 2. days 3. funnies 4. ponies

B. 1. valleys 2. toys 3. babies 4. beauties 5. trays

C. 1. don-keys 2. mon-keys 3. sto-ries
4. de-lays 5. li-brar-ies

Page 158

A. 1. days 2. libraries 3. funnies 4. stories
5. monkeys 6. pennies 7. toys 8. beauties
9. trays 10. ponies 11. babies 12. delays
13. valleys 14. donkeys

Unit 27

Page 163

A. 1. copied 2. replied
3. carried 4. married

B. 1. copying 2. staying
3. replying 4. carrying
5. playing 6. enjoying
7. marrying

C. 1. stay 2. play
3. enjoy 4. play
5. carry 6. reply

D. 1. carried 2. married
3. carrying 4. marrying

Page 164

A. 1. cop-ied 2. cop-y-ing 3. re-ply-ing
4. mar-ried 5. re-plied 6. car-ry-ing
7. en-joy-ing 8. mar-ry-ing 9. car-ried

B. 1. stayed 2. playing 3. enjoyed

C. 1. carried 2. copied 3. married 4. replied

Page 165

A. 1. married 2. marrying 3. copied 4. copying
5. replied 6. staying 7. carried 8. carrying
9. playing 10. played 11. enjoying 12. enjoyed

Unit 28

Page 170

A. 1. shaped   2. chased
    3. raced   4. shaping
    5. chasing 6. racing

B. 1. deciding decided
    2. noticing noticed
    3. forcing   forced
    4. creasing creased

C. 1. noticed   2. noticing

D. 1. raced   2. decided
    3. noticed   4. forced
    5. racing   6. deciding
    7. noticing 8. forcing

Page 171

A. 1. shaped   2. racing   3. creased   4. forced
    5. deciding 6. noticed   7. chasing

B. 1. noticing 2. chased   3. shaping   4. decided
    5. forcing   6. raced   7. creasing

C. 1. deciding 2. creasing

Page 172

A. 1. raced   2. racing   3. noticed   4. creased
    5. shaped   6. chasing   chased   7. decided   8. forcing
    9. shaping   10. deciding   11. creasing   12. forced
    13. noticing

319

Unit 29

Page 177
A. 1. braver   2. bravest   B. 1. larger   largest
                              2. finer   finest
                              3. nicer   nicest

C. 1. bigger   biggest   D. 1. madder   2. fatter
   2. madder   maddest   3. maddest   4. fattest

E. 1. nicer   2. nicest

Page 178
A. 1. larg-er   2. brav-er   3. big-ger   4. mad-der
   5. fin-er   6. fat-ter   7. nic-er

B. 1. biggest   2. bravest   3. fattest   4. finest
   5. largest   6. maddest   7. nicest

Page 179
A. 1. larger   2. largest   3. nicer   4. nicest
   5. braver   6. bravest   7. madder   8. maddest
   9. bigger   10. biggest   11. fatter 12. fattest
   13. finer   14. finest

320

Spelling Review 30- 4th grade
(answers)

Part 1	Part 2	Part 3	Part 4
1. C	1. B	1. A	1. A
2. A	2. A	2. B	2. B
3. C	3. B	3. A	3. B
4. B	4. C	4. C	4. C
5. B	5. C	5. C	5. C
6. A	6. A	6. B	6. A
7. C	7. B	7. A	7. B
8. A	8. A	8. B	8. A
9. B	9. C	9. C	9. C
10. B	10. B	10. A	10. A
11. A	11. A	11. C	11. B
12. C	12. C	12. B	12. C
13. C	13. B	13. C	13. B
14. A	14. C	14. B	14. A
15. B	15. A	15. B	15. B
16. B	16. A	16. A	16. C
17. C	17. C	17. C	17. A
18. A	18. B		

Unit 31

Page 185

A. 1. they'd 2. you'd
 3. who'd 4. he'd
 5. I'd 6. she'd
 7. how'd

B. 1. we'll 2. they'll
 3. she'll

C. 1. doesn't 2. aren't

D. 1. what's 2. who's

Page 186

A. 1. what's 2. she'd 3. how'd 4. she'll
 5. we'll 6. they'll 7. who'd 8. they'd
 9. he'd 10. you'd 11. doesn't 12. who's
 13. I'd 14. aren't

B. 1. who'd 2. how'd 3. they'd
 4. doesn't 5. she'd

Page 187

A. 1. Who'd 2. Who's 3. I'd 4. You'd
 5. aren't 6. what's 7. they'd 8. we'll
 9. Doesn't 10. He'd 11. she'd 12. she'll
 13. they'd 14. How'd

Unit 32

Page 192
A. 1. sail 2. mail   B. 1. tale 2. male
   3. wood 4. sum   3. sale
   5. horse 6. tail
   7. beet

C. 1. horse 2. beet

Page 193
A. 1. sum   2. male   3. sail   4. mail
   5. tale 6. horse 7. beat   8. hoarse
   9. beet

B. 1. sale 2. some   3. tail
   4. wood 5. would

C. 1. adj. 2. verb   3. adj.   4. noun

Page 194
A. 1. Would   sum   2. some   mail
   3. hoarse   4. horse   tail
   5. sail   6. wood
   7. sale   8. tale
   9. beet   10. male
   11. beat

Unit 33

Page 199
A. 1. telephone 2. dolphin
   3. photo   4. phonics
   5. nephew   6. orphan
   7. paragraph 8. phrase
   9. pamphlet

B. 1. cough   2. tough
   3. rough   4. laugh
   5. enough

C. 1. dolphin   2. photo
   3. phonics   4. nephew
   5. orphan   6. enough
   7. pamphlet

D. 1. telephone   2. paragraph

Page 200
A. 1. telephone 2. tough   3. phrase
   4. cough   5. laugh   6. rough

B. 1. photo   2. phonics   3. orphan   4. enough
   5. dolphin   6. paragraph 7. nephew   8. pamphlet

C. 1. adj.   2. verb   3. noun   4. noun

Page 201
A. 1. rough   2. nephew   3. laugh   4. tough

B. 1. telephone 2. pamphlet 3. paragraph 4. orphan
   5. cough   6. photo   7. phonics   8. enough
   9. phrase   10. dolphin

Unit 34

Page 206
A. 1. enjoyable 2. available
3. acceptable

B. 1. disturbance 2. insurance
3. assistance

C. 1. shortage 2. baggage
3. passage 4. postage

D. 1. wooden 2. sadden

E. 1. tiresome 2. wholesome

Page 207
A. 1. en-joy-a-ble 2. dis-turb-ance 3. short-age 4. bag-gage
5. pas-sage 6. a-vail-a-ble 7. post-age 8. ac-cept-a-ble
9. in-sur-ance 10. as-sist-ance 11. wood-en 12. sad-den
13. tiresome 14. wholesome

B. 1. acceptable 3. available
2. assistance 4. insurance

Page 208
A. 1. postage 2. shortage 3. saddened 4. wholesome
5. assistance 6. disturbance 7. enjoyable 8. passage
9. insurance 10. available 11. tiresome 12. acceptable
13. wooden 14. baggage

325

Unit 35

Page 213
A. 1. payment   2. statement   B. 1. goodness   2. darkness
   3. equipment   3. needless

C. 1. thankful   2. restful   D. 1. needless   2. hopeless
   3. peaceful   4. careful
   5. cheerful

E. equipment

F. 1. spotless   2. statement

Page 214
A. 1. careful   2. cheerful   3. darkness   4. equipment
   5. goodness   6. hopeless   7. kindness   8. needless
   9. payment   10. peaceful   11. restful   12. spotless
   13. statement   14. thankful

B. 1. careful   2. cheerful   3. peaceful   4. darkness
   5. kindness   6. statement   7. needless

Page 215
A. 1. restful   2. careful   darkness   3. needless
   4. thankful   goodness 5. peaceful   6. equipment
   7. spotless   8. kindness   9. payment
   10. statement   11. cheerful   12. hopeless

Spelling Review 36- 4th grade
(answers)

Part 1	Part 2	Part 3	Part 4
1. B	1. C	1. A	1. B
2. A	2. B	2. B	2. C
3. C	3. A	3. A	3. C
4. A	4. B	4. C	4. A
5. C	5. A	5. C	5. B
6. C	6. A	6. B	6. A
7. A	7. C	7. B	7. B
8. B	8. B	8. A	8. C
9. A	9. C	9. C	9. A
10. C	10. A	10. B	10. C
11. B	11. C	11. B	11. B
12. B	12. B	12. C	12. B
13. C	13. B	13. A	13. A
14. A	14. A	14. B	14. A
15. A	15. C	15. C	15. C
16. B	16. B	16. A	16. B
17. C	17. C	17. B	17. B
18. A	18. A		

www.ingramcontent.com/pod-product-compliance
Lightning Source LLC
Chambersburg PA
CBHW080332170426
43194CB00014B/2531